COMBAT PISTOLS

COMBAT PISTOLS

A manual of modern handguns

TERRY GANDER

Sterling Publishing Co., Inc. New York

Cover illustration by Robert Partridge

10 9 8 7 6 5 4 3 2 1

Published in 1990 by Sterling Publishing Co., Inc.
387 Park Avenue South, New York, N.Y. 10016
Published in Great Britain by Patrick Stephens Ltd,
part of the Thorsens Publishing Group. © 1989 by Terry Gander
Distributed in Canada by Sterling Publishing
% Canadian Manda Group, P.O. Box 920, Station U
Toronto, Ontario, Canada M8Z 5P9
Manufactured in the United States of America
Sterling ISBN 0-8069-7334-X Paper

CONTENTS

INTRODUCTION

One of the most surprising aspects of the modern combat pistol is that it has managed to survive into today's military world. Over the last fifty years or so, numerous attempts have been made to 'finally' acknowledge the limitations of the service pistol and consign it to the dustbin of small arms technical history, and yet it has survived. Indeed, today it thrives in numerous forms, still the object of the small arms designer's art and the end product of a great deal of production effort.

Exactly why the pistol has survived is fairly easy to explain: there is, at present, nothing to replace it. The numerous attempts to replace the pistol with some other form of weapon have all come to naught. Perhaps the most extreme attempt was by the Americans during the Second World War. Acknowledging that their service pistol, the .45 M1911, was of doubtful combat or any other value, except in extreme cases, the American military authorities developed the weapon that became the M1 Carbine. M1 Carbines were churned out by the million, but they never did replace the M1911. That venerable automatic continued to serve on despite them, and does so to this day, while the M1 Carbine has long since been declared obsolete by most

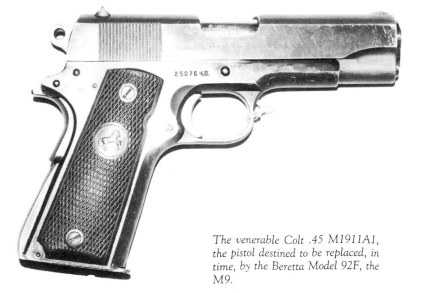

The venerable Colt .45 M1911A1, the pistol destined to be replaced, in time, by the Beretta Model 92F, the M9.

military organizations and is now regarded merely as an odd dead-end of weapon development.

The same fate has not yet befallen the sub-machine gun. When the sub-machine gun was introduced on a large scale during the Second World War, many military pundits saw it as a viable alternative to the pistol and issued the new weapons accordingly. The sub-machine gun has made considerable inroads into what had once been pistol territory, but the pistol has still managed to remain, with its rate of issue largely unchanged. The sub-machine gun has instead developed into a weapon form in its own right.

One other anticipated threat to the pistol has also been consigned to the oddity bracket. That is the machine-pistol (or machine-carbine), which continues to appear in modern forms, as these pages will show, but is now seen as an odd hybrid lacking many of the attributes of the pistol or its larger relative, the sub-machine gun.

Exactly why no viable alternative to the pistol has been developed requires several answers. Despite its general lack of power, a very short effective range, an inherent lack of accuracy other than in skilled hands, and relatively high unit cost, the pistol still has many operational and non-operational roles. These are largely dictated by the better points of the service pistol. It is small and light enough to be carried for extended periods without causing excessive bother to the carrier, and it can be carried relatively safely, also for extended periods, and can always be ready for immediate use.

Set against these attributes there are few defined operational roles for the pistol to play on the modern battlefield. These roles are nearly all confined to personnel who have to carry a pistol for the simple reason that they cannot carry any other weapon due to the nature of their duties. Two examples that immediately spring to mind are the drivers and other crew members of armoured vehicles, who simply do not have the space to carry anything larger than a pistol. This has not prevented some armed forces from issuing sub-machine guns to armoured and other vehicle crews, but many armies continue to use the pistol. The other easily-recognized category includes signallers and other specialists who have to carry heavy or bulky loads on their backs and thus have a very limited capability to carry anything larger or heavier than a pistol.

Pistols par excellence, the SIG pistol range: from the back, the P230 with another P230 in its holster; the central pistol is a P220 with a P225 on the far right; the pistol in the foreground is a P226.

Another category is that of military police personnel, who often have only a limited capacity to carry weapons larger than a pistol or sub-machine gun when operating close to the front line. This leads us to what is probably the largest military pistol-using category, namely the guard duty and security unit personnel who have to carry out their various duties away from operational areas and yet who still have to carry some form of weapon to defend themselves and their locality. Military police again come into this category, but there are also the various staff personnel at the many headquarters and logistic function points. Many armed forces equip such personnel with standard rifles but others have acknowledged that the drivers of trucks or combat engineer equipment have little space or freedom to carry a bulky service rifle with them at all times, and so the pistol is issued instead.

It is with military police and security unit users that the pistol is perhaps at its best. Within many armed forces, the pistol strapped to a belt is a badge of the military policeman, and it is with such units that the pistol probably finds its most valuable military role. The pistol can be carried by such personnel for extended periods without undue worry, but it is always ready for immediate use if needed. Even in this role, the pistol's limited range is often a drawback, but set against that, the pistol is better than no weapon at all. This role also highlights something that continues to remain one of the service pistol's biggest assets.

In many circumstances, both in and out of a military operational area, the very carrying or brandishing of a pistol imparts authority to the user. In this way the pistol acts as a badge for the carrier or handler, who can use it to impose his command on others. It is for this reason that many military police units carry pistols, as mentioned above, and why personnel in unfriendly rear areas continue to carry pistols at all times, both on and off duty. Their pistols act as a mark of authority, but they also impart a sense of security to the carrier. Even though the user may be the world's worst shot, he still knows that he has a lethal weapon at his command and can use its potential should it ever be required.

Cut-away parts list of a typical modern revolver, in this case the Ruger Police Service-Six, the numbers refer to spare parts.

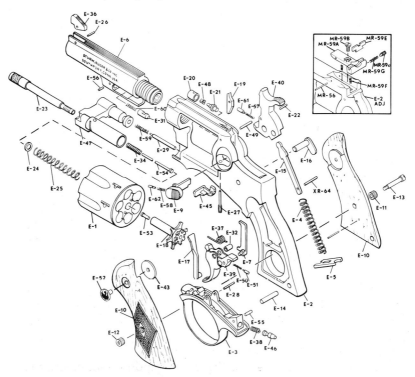

The criminal (or terrorist) can also use the pistol for very similar reasons. By waving around a pistol when making demands, or using a pistol to impose his (or her) will on a situation, a criminal is only taking the 'badge of authority syndrome' one stage further, with the hapless victim(s) knowing all too well the consequences should they not be compliant.

The badge of authority syndrome is another reason why many staff officers continue to carry pistols, even though they may be unlikely ever to use them in a combat situation. Their pistol denotes rank and also provides a measure of self-assurance to the wearer. However, it is noticeable that few present-day high-ranking officers carry pistols once they reach front-line areas. Instead they are likely to carry a rifle or some such weapon, knowing only too well that snipers will be keeping an eye open for targets who appear to be in a position of authority; the wearing of a pistol often denotes a likely target.

Special forces continue to be one of the pistol's more important operational users, no matter what form the special forces involved might take. One of the most conspicuous facts regarding special forces units, from frogmen to free-fall parachutists, is that they have to carry a great deal of equipment with them. That may leave room for only the pistol as a personal weapon. There are some special forces operational scenarios where the selection of a pistol will be the only possible course of action, and in some circumstances only a silenced model will suffice.

Other potential pistol-users include aircrew operating over hostile territory, as well as boat handlers in maritime or amphibious situations. But time and time again, compiling a list of potential pistol-users leads to rear area guard and security units. This in its turn leads us to civilian users and police forces.

No apologies will be made for including police forces in a book dealing with the modern combat pistol. Nearly every police force in the world carries pistols at some time or another, and some carry pistols all the time. This may be seen as a reflection of the state of society in which people live or as a measure of the capabilities that law-breakers can draw upon to support their criminal activities. In some parts of the world the constant battle between the law enforcement agencies and law breakers has grown to a state of open warfare and to a point where lethal weapons are constantly in use by both sides.

For law officers, the pistol is the ideal weapon. Once again, the pistol's small dimensions and light weight enable it to be carried either in an overt holster or concealed about the person, but ready for use at all times. The point was reached long ago where police officers had to attain a high level of pistol-handling skills to remain qualified to carry hand guns on duty. We are now at the point where many civilian police units can maintain a standard of all-round pistol proficiency much higher than the military personnel who might expect to use the pistol during combat on a battlefield.

Police forces must therefore overcome one of the pistol's major drawbacks. It takes a long time to teach a recruit how to use a pistol properly and safely. Few military organizations have the necessary time to teach all potential pistol-users even the essential pistol basics, but most police forces, usually having only one type of weapon to deal with, can find time to divert officers to training sessions where pistol skills can be imparted or refreshed at regular intervals.

Needless to say, the pistol-manufacturing concerns have accordingly produced pistols specifically for police users, but while there are specialist police pistols (the ASP and the Heckler & Koch P7 pistols are obvious examples) the line between military and police pistols is becoming increasingly blurred. Many police forces simply utilize the standard service pistols used by their national armed forces. Others go their own way, but if there is a definite statement that can be made regarding any difference between police and military pistols, it is that until recently most police forces favoured revolvers, while the military plumped for the automatic.

The difference between the revolver and the automatic was clear at one time during the automatic pistol's development. The automatic was the more complex weapon of the two, was more prone to stoppages at awkward moments, often took time to bring into action and always required far more maintenance. That point was passed many years ago, and today the automatic is as reliable as the revolver, is as easy and rapid to bring into use as the revolver and requires no more maintenance either. We are now at the stage where the automatic pistol can be made smaller and easier to conceal or carry, and it is as safe to handle as the inherently safe revolver. One point where the automatic scores heavily over the revolver is in the amount of ready-use ammunition that can be carried in the weapon. Nearly all revolvers are

Revolver technology at its most extreme. This is the Ruger Super Redhawk, a .44 Magnum revolver intended for the shooting enthusiast and even the game hunter. This example has a 241 mm barrel and a Ruger Integral Scope Mounting.

limited by their cylinder dimensions to five or six rounds, but some automatics can carry up to 17 rounds (as with the Glock 17), plus an extra round in the chamber ready to fire.

All these advances in automatic pistol design have not led to the complete demise of the revolver. Hollywood is constantly reminding us that many American police forces, and especially plain-clothes operatives, still favour the revolver, whereas their European counterparts have for long favoured automatics.

The last few decades have seen a dramatic improvement in the overall safety standards of the automatic. Many of the older automatic pistol designs embodied only token safety mechanisms, and were prone to go off if dropped or handled clumsily. The modern automatic pistol is a very different weapon that encapsulates all manner of ingenious methods of preventing unwanted firings. That has not meant that they have to be extensively fiddled with once they are needed in a hurry. Many of the latest pistols require no more preparation for firing after loading, other than simply squeezing the trigger in exactly the same manner as a conventional revolver. At all other times they can be carried holding a ready-to-use round already chambered, in complete safety, with only the human factor remaining as a safety hazard.

Along with the improvements in safety devices, the modern combat pistol has seen some other recent changes. One obvious change has been in the ammunition fired. At the turn of the century, virtually every new pistol introduced on to the market had its own specific calibre, and could fire only the ammunition that was produced for that particular model. Time, experience and commercial impositions have gradually whittled away the array of calibres and ammunition types, to the point where today only a few remain.

Of those few, one calibre and ammunition type is dominant; the 9 x 19 mm Parabellum cartridge. It is not a new cartridge, having started life back in 1902 when it was developed to be the ammunition for the famous Luger pistol*. Gradually the use of the 9 mm Parabellum round spread, to the point where it is now the universal pistol cartridge of the Western bloc. Even the American armed forces have decided to adopt it in place of their equally venerable .45 ACP (Automatic Colt Pistol) although it will be a very long time before the .45 cartridge is finally laid to rest.

The almost universal use of the 9 x 19 mm Parabellum cartridge should indicate that the term 9 mm Parabellum denotes some form of standard. In broad terms this is true. The 9 mm Parabellum is a standard NATO cartridge, and strict standards are laid down regarding dimensions, materials, and so on. However, these standards are more often used as guidelines only; many manufacturers deviate from the standards a great deal. Thus there are 9 mm Parabellum cartridges and 9 mm Parabellum cartridges. There are 9 mm Parabellum cartridges that use propellant loads that are definitely 'hot', and firing them will stress some pistol frames to their limits. Others are decidedly underpowered and will not function reliably and consistently in every make of pistol. Some use metal- or nylon-jacketed bullets, while others are bare lead. Some bullet noses are blunt, others are streamlined, and some manufacturers produce bullets with hollow points. Even the cartridge cases vary from thin light alloy to more substantial brass constructions. The overall quality standard might vary from the barely adequate to the excellent.

The variations are introduced by many factors. One is very obviously price. Quality ammunition costs money, and some manufacturers cater for the lower end of the market for the simple reason that they lack the technology to produce anything better; others are quite the opposite. There is also the factor that 9 mm Parabellum cartridges are not produced solely for pistols. They are also used in sub-machine guns.

* The Luger is not included in the scope of this book, as it cannot be said to fall in the category of 'modern' combat pistols. It is still in production, but only for the benefit of collectors and enthusiasts.

Generally speaking, 9 mm Parabellum rounds intended for sub-machine gun use are better made and have more powerful propellant loads, making their employment in pistols a somewhat risky business. Some manufacturers go to the length of producing armour-piercing or semi-armour-piercing Parabellum rounds for use with sub-machine guns. Such cartridges, again speaking generally, should not be fired from pistols.

Thus the 9 mm Parabellum cartridge cannot be regarded as a standard cartridge, even though at first sight it should be. There are too many variations, which is perhaps not so remarkable, considering the number of countries in which 9 mm Parabellum ammunition is produced. These vary from Greece and India to Finland and Egypt. Nine mm Parabellum ammunition is even produced behind the Iron Curtain, for both Hungary and Czechoslovakia manufacture 9 mm Parabellum for export sales.

The 9 mm Parabellum cartridge is primarily a military round. Police forces tend to favour slightly less powerful rounds, for in many police situations the extra power is not required or could even be undesirable (e.g. by penetrating walls and causing casualties to innocent bystanders). Thus calibres such as 7.65 mm and 0.38 are still widely used by many police forces. This has not prevented the introduction of super-powerful cartridges and weapons to fire them. The super-powerful cartridges include the

The Colt Delta Elite, a rework of the old Colt M1911A1 Government Model to accommodate the 10 mm Auto cartridge.

One of the very latest Ruger revolvers, the Ruger GP-100 .357 Magnum. This revolver has cushioned grip panels that are anatomically designed to sit well in the hand, and the ejector shroud under the barrel is elongated to make the pistol slightly muzzle-heavy, to produce a steadier hold.

Magnums in calibres such as 0.357, 0.41 and 0.44, but they were not developed primarily for police users or the military. They were developed via another route, the pistol enthusiast.

The pistol enthusiast is a complex beast who varies from the target shooter who loads his own ammunition to the information ferret who has no desire or opportunity to actually own a gun. They are a sizeable market, even for the large pistol producers, for however many restrictions are placed upon pistol ownership, as they are in many countries, there are still enough pistol enthusiasts willing to pay for the pleasure of actually owning and firing a pistol. Therefore manufacturers produce pistols and ammunition for them.

All manner of pistols are produced to cater specifically for the sporting pistol enthusiast, with 'sporting' a term that covers a wide field which varies from small calibre single-shot pistols, used for what the Americans call 'plinking', to massive bolt-action hand guns firing rifle ammunition and used for big game hunting. Few pistols used by such enthusiasts fall into the combat pistol category, as do even fewer of the highly refined and expensive target shooting pistols.

That still leaves the shooting enthusiast who devotes his spare time to handling and firing combat weapons. Few of them ever expect to use their treasured pistols against anything other than paper targets. For many of them, the firing is only an adjunct of their pastime. They are interested in the technical aspects of combat pistols, and that means everything from delving into the finer points of muzzle velocities and muzzle energies, to determining the optimum shape of a butt grip. Others, including those who may never even handle a gun, become involved in historical points or gathering information on rare sub-variants. There is also a very wide band of pistol enthusiasts who simply want to own or make the biggest bang possible.

This is the realm of the hand-loaders. Since few can aspire to actually manufacturing their own hand guns (although home modifications are another matter) the only alternative is to hand load their own ammunition. This activity can be as harmless as attempting to keep down shooting costs, while for others it means attempting to pack as much propellant into a cartridge as is feasible without causing the pistol involved to explode when fired. The hand-loading chapter has grown considerably over the years, especially in the United States where commercial ammunition producers eventually found it worth their while to produce the super-powerful Magnum cartridges, and pistol manufacturers produced pistols (usually revolvers) to fire them.

It was not long before police forces found the Magnum pistols to be very useful weapons - but only in trained hands. Firing any of the Magnum cartridges is something of an experience. The muzzle blast is prodigious, the flash can be severe and the recoil is considerable. The effects of what are often blunt-nosed bullets on a target are dreadful: even a peripheral hit on the human frame will produce traumatic effects that can cause severe shock and internal damage. The Magnum rounds are not to be trifled with.

Military use of Magnum rounds has been largely confined to police and security forces. Placing such weapons in the hands of barely-trained military personnel would be counter-productive, not only in safety terms but in the reactions of trainees to the awe-inspiring firing noise and recoil. Many American servicemen still speak in awe of the day they first encountered the .45 M1911 pistol during their basic training. Many will freely admit that they were terrified of the things, and still are. Some manage to overcome their initial aprehensions and proceed to learn how to handle the M1911 and other pistols properly - others do not.

Nine mm pistols are scarcely less awe-inspiring, but, generally speaking, they are easier to handle and are effective enough for most military purposes. The 9 mm Parabellum round, despite having a lighter bullet than the old .45 ACP, manages to have better penetration powers and produces enough energy to make targets alter the nature of their activities. It also has a considerable range. Despite operational ranges being short (25 metres is usually regarded as the upper combat limit, although really skilled shots can expect to hit a human-sized target at 200 metres five times out of ten) the 9 mm Parabellum bullet is capable of inflicting wounds that could be fatal, out to a range of 2,000 metres or thereabouts.

Yet there are still those who want to go one better. Once again, the American pistol enthusiast has been busy seeking that something extra, and two new super-powerful cartridges have recently appeared on the scene. As yet, there are few pistols that can fire them, but some are imminent.

One of these new cartridges is known as the 10 mm Auto, which appears to have everything – more muzzle energy, a higher muzzle velocity, and so on. What it does not appear to have is a viable military future, for it is another of those rounds that is simply too powerful for the task. The 10 mm Auto has entered the realm of pocket artillery, and while there are pistol enthusiasts for whom the 10 mm Auto will act as a form of Holy Grail, there are few military users who will even contemplate the introduction of a new super-powerful cartridge, when existing cartridges are doing all that is required, to say nothing of procuring new weapons to fire the new ammunition.

To date, there have been few pistols available to fire the 10 mm Auto. There is a series of automatics known as the 'Bren Tens' that are obviously produced for the enthusiast, but the only remotely large-scale production to date has been of a variant of the old Colt M1911, sold under the Colt label as the Delta Elite.

A more viable cartridge can be seen in the form of the .41 Auto Express. The design of this one has been far more carefully thought out, and the overall dimensions of the bullet and cartridge case are almost identical to those of the 9 x 19 mm Parabellum - the case is marginally longer. Thus to produce the new cartridge on existing machinery would not involve many changes, and the same can be said for the weapons that fire the new round. To convert an existing pistol to fire .41 Auto Express, modifications need be made only to the barrel, magazine and possibly the sights. That is quite a different prospect from having to procure an entirely new pistol.

By all accounts the .41 Auto Express appears to have a bright future. A version of the Israeli Desert Eagle has already been produced to fire the new round, and other pistols are on the way. Whether or not the military will find the .41 Auto Express a viable round remains to be seen, but it seems unlikely. The 9 mm Parabellum is so well entrenched that it will take an extraordinary ammunition innovation to make any form of impact on military procurement circles.

Included in this book is a cross-section of modern combat pistols. It is not an encyclopaedia of the genre, for to attempt that would take years and the end result would still be incomplete. The most important message of this book is that the modern combat pistol is alive and kicking, to an extent that continues to confound the prophets and pundits who pop up every now and again to declare that the combat pistol is obsolete and should be done away with. Every year new pistol models appear, new ammunition is devised, and all the while old models are updated and modified into new forms and for new markets. It all makes for a fascinating subject for study, and a rewarding one.

No one can ever think that they know everything about modern combat pistols. We can only go on researching and learning more about combat pistols every year.

GLOCK 17

Nation of origin: Austria
Ammunition: 9 x 19 mm
Operation: short recoil
Weight: 0.87 kg
Length: 188 mm
Length of barrel: 114 mm
Magazine capacity: 17 rounds
Muzzle velocity: approx 350 m/s

The Austrian Glock 17 is one of the more unusual pistols in service today and it is one that gained a certain notoriety, even before it became widely known. The main reason for this notoriety comes from the nature of the Glock 17's innovative construction, as the one-piece sliding receiver is made from a high impact polymer material. Having heard of this non-metallic material, some media personnel have seen fit to announce that the Glock 17 is a 'plastic pistol' that will pass through metal detectors without notice. This has led to some calls for its bann-

The Glock 17; 40 per cent of this very advanced military pistol is manufactured from non-metallic polymer materials.

ing from sale, to prevent ownership by unauthorized persons who, according to some news media text peddlers, could carry the pistol on board aircraft undetected, and thus make possible a new round of terrorist hijackings and other crimes. Needless to say, such claims for undetectability by the usual round of metal sensor systems are unfounded. The Glock 17 merely happens to have a lower metal content than most similar weapons, and will still show up on X-ray machines, metal detectors and all the usual array of sensor devices now likely to be encountered at airports and in many public buildings. All the same, the use of high impact polymers where metals have previously been employed in pistol construction is relatively novel, and would seem to indicate a path that other small-arms designers might well follow in the future. The polymer used in the Glock 17 is as well capable of withstanding the shocks and knocks of service use as the metals and light alloys used in other weapons, and is less expensive overall to produce in its final form.

The incorporation of the polymer reciever apart, the Glock 17 is still a very advanced weapon. It is a well-made automatic pistol with a smooth outline and uses a minimum of parts (only 33 in total). It can be field stripped for repair or maintenance in less than a minute, using only a simple pin or even the sharp point of a nail. The breech is positively locked at the instant of firing, using the widely-applied Colt-Browning cam-controlled dropping barrel principle.

There is no safety catch system in the usual sense, for the weapon will only fire after a definite and prolonged pressure on the trigger. The first pressure on the trigger releases a trigger safety mechanism only after the trigger has moved back about 5 mm. The striker is not cocked until after even more pressure, and yet more pressure is needed before two further safeties (one holding the firing pin in a firm lock) are removed. Thus only when a definite trigger pressure has been applied will all safety and cocking operations allow the striker to fall on to the cartridge for firing. As the trigger is released, all the safeties fall back into the 'safe' condition ready for the next trigger pressure, safety and firing sequence to begin all over again.

Despite all these safeties being reliant on positive trigger pressure, actually firing the Glock 17 is easy, and the trigger operation is smooth and positive. The trigger pressure itself can

One Austrian pistol that did not make it, the Steyr GB. This advanced pistol had several unusual features such as an 18-round magazine and polygonal rifling inside the chromed barrel. However the pistol proved to be difficult to manufacture in bulk and therefore rather expensive. Sales were limited and production has now ceased.

be adjusted by the user (within limits) to suit himself, but the minimum pressure is 2 kg.

One item to note regarding the Glock 17 is the butt. This is quite a large component, but it fits into the average hand with ease and provides a good and comfortable firing grip. The large size is made necessary by the generous magazine capacity, which is no less than 17 standard NATO 9 mm rounds. This measure of ammunition capacity would be quite an asset in any shooting situation, and it must be the largest ammunition capacity of any conventional pistol in use today. The weight in the butt also tends to make the pistol's balance stay well back into the hand, which many pistol users will find an advantage. The Glock 17 can be readily aimed and fired using only one hand, but many firers favour the two-handed grip for accuracy and control, and for them the Glock 17 has a pronounced reverse arc to accommodate the extra finger(s) on the front portion of the trigger guard; this is a feature shared by many other pistols.

Needless to say, the Glock 17 has attracted quite a bit of attention, quite apart from that bestowed by the lay Press. Almost as soon as the Glock 17 appeared during the early 1980s, it was accepted for service by the Austrian Army, who were soon followed by the Austrian Police. They were later followed by other

European police forces and the type was a natural for the various special forces and paramilitary units of several nations. A large order came from the Norwegian Army, and other NATO nations have examined the Glock 17 with an eye to re-equipping their armed forces. It is possible that the Glock 17 will be one of the pistols to be considered should the United States Army ever carry out the threatened rerun of the selection contest for their M9 pistol (the M9 requirement has already been met by the Beretta 92F - q.v.). The one aspect of the Glock 17 that does not meet the M9 specification is that it lacks a double action external hammer system, demonstrating that in some ways the Glock 17 designers are already far ahead of the competition. The Glock 17 quite simply does not need the external mechanism thought to be essential by the Americans; its safety and firing mechanisms are good enough to do without such a feature.

The impact of the Glock 17 on the pistol scene has been profound enough to make many small-arms authorities state that the weapon is currently the best all-round service pistol in the world. Anyone trying to counter that sort of statement will have to muster some very good arguments to the contrary.

FN BROWNING HIGH-POWER

Nation of origin: Belgium
Ammunition: 9 x 19 mm
Operation: short recoil
Weight: loaded 1.1 kg
Length: 197 mm
Length of barrel: 120 mm
Magazine capacity: 13 rounds
Muzzle velocity: approx. 350 m/s

When considering the FN Browning High-Power pistol, one has to remember that it is a design that dates back to 1925, when John Moses Browning turned his hand to designing a pistol that could be deemed an advance over other pistol designs of that time, including his M1911, designed when he worked with Colts. It was 1935 before the new pistol actually went into production at the Fabrique Nationale (FN) plant at Herstal, near Liège, and the High-Power has not been out of production since then.

There is no sign that the venerable High-Power will ever pass out of production or service in the foreseeable future. It is in ser-

The 9 mm Browning High-Power, one of the most widely-used of all present-day combat pistols.

A British military policeman practising on the ranges with his Browning High-Power pistol.

vice with the armed forces of well over 50 nations and is likely to be encountered in virtually any part of the world. High-Powers even turned up during the 1982 Falkland Islands campaign, when numbers of examples that had been licence-produced in Argentina fell into British hands. During the Second World War, the type was produced in Canada and many of them were sent to China, where they still crop up from time to time. Between 1939 and 1945 the High-Power was used by both sides in Europe (the Germans using captured examples and more that were turned out for their own forces using captured production facilities in Belgium); the British used Canadian-produced examples. The British Armed Forces continue to use the High-Power as their standard service pistol; it is designated the 9 mm Pistol Automatic L9A1.

Over the years the High-Power has been given many names. Originally it was known as the Model 1935, but it has been known as the HP (for High Power) and the GP (Grand Puissance). It has also appeared in many forms, from a basic service pistol with no frills, fixed sights and a simple finish, to refinements such as a wooden holster that doubles as a butt to convert the weapon into a form of single-shot carbine. Other embellishments have included complex sights, high quality finishes, commemorative and engraved 'editions', and changes to the trigger mechanism to permit fully automatic fire. There have been lightened versions with various items cut away or replaced by lighter materials, and even some rather odd variants (that were not very successful commercially) that have attenuated butts and shortened barrels to enable them to be used as undercover 'pocket' pistols. Many other variants have been produced, but the above listing covers the main types.

Exactly why the High-Power has been so successful over the years is not difficult to determine, for by many accounts it is the service pistol *par excellence*. It is robust, reliable and safe to an extent that many other pistols can only aspire to. Good as the original Colt M1911 design was, John Browning took his design principles one stage further and produced a pistol that continues to use his falling-barrel locking system allied to a cam to produce an even better design mechanically. The cam modification also proved to be easier to manufacture and is less prone to wear over a long period of use. By adopting the widely-favoured 9 mm Parabellum cartridge, not only did the Browning design become more attractive to many users outside the United States, but the cartridge dimensions made it possible to pack no fewer than 13 rounds into the box magazine. At the time of its introduction, a 13-round magazine capacity was quite a combat innovation, and it is still a feature that appeals to many soldiers.

The external hammer is also a carry-over from the M1911 and it remains as useful with the High-Power as it does with the M1911. The user has a definite indication of the state of readiness of his pistol, and if the worst comes to the worst and a misfire occurs, the hammer can be recocked ready for another attempt at firing.

The weight of the High-Power can be something of a hurdle to the novice pistol user, and the pistol is something of a handful for the untrained. Once the weight and bulk of the weapon have become more familiar, the High-Power can prove itself to be an accurate and reliable weapon at the usual pistol combat ranges, and the strength of the weapon is such that, if all else fails, the pistol can still be used as a club. It is unlikely to be used as a missile, for many military High-Powers make use of that most useful of military attachments, the lanyard. This is connected to a ring at the base of the butt to prevent the pistol being snatched away from the owner at close quarters, and also keeps the pistol connected to the user, should it be dropped.

Having listed the attributes of the High-Power, it would be as well to mention some of its shortcomings. One is the absence of the various sophisticated safeties that are now commonplace on more modern designs. The main safety is the usual slide catch, and there is a barrel locking device that ensures that the pistol will not fire if the slide is not fully home or if the magazine is not in position. There is also a notch (known as a half-bent) on the hammer which ensures that the cocked pistol will not fire if it is accidentally dropped on to its muzzle. If this happens, the sear will engage the hammer notch and ensure that the hammer does not fall on to the firing pin. Instead, it falls into a safe 'half cock' position.

Perhaps the biggest drawback for many is the pistol's weight and bulk, but again this can be turned to advantage by the robustness and reliability that comes with solid construction, although several attempts have been made to lighten the design over the years. But the bulk of the weapon is such that many users find it difficult to use accurately at anything other than

A commercial version of the Browning High-Power fitted with ramp rear sights.

very short ranges. To counter that, many experienced pistol users swear that the High-Power is more accurate than many others, quoting the weight of a full magazine in the wide butt that makes for a steadying factor when aiming. So perhaps the answer to the weight and bulk problem is a modicum of training.

While pistol buffs are happy to argue the demerits and merits of any pistol, one thing is certain. The High-Power is in widespread use all over the world and there is no sign of its being replaced by anything else. Production continues at Herstal, and the latest production model has some up-dating features, such as revised grip plates for a more comfortable hold, wider sights that are easier and quicker to use in action, an ambidextrous safety catch and an anti-glare plating finish. There is also a slightly revised series derived from the High-Power that includes the shortened version mentioned in the text. While this model continues to use the 9 x 19 mm Parabellum cartridge, its magazine holds only seven rounds.

TYPE 80

Nation of origin: People's Republic of China
Ammunition: 7.62 x 25 mm Tokarev
Operation: recoil
Weight: with 10-round magazine, 1.1 kg
Length: 300 mm
Length of barrel: approx 140 mm
Magazine capacity: 10 or 20 rounds
Muzzle velocity: 470 m/s
Rate of fire: burst, cyclic, 60 rpm

Over the years, the Chinese small-arms industry has churned out a surprising array of pistols. Many of them have been direct copies of existing weapons, such as the still-produced Type 54 which is a direct and unashamed copy of the Soviet Tokarev TT-33. Other pistols, especially between the wars, have been of doubtful workmanship and quality, but those days are now long gone and modern production Chinese pistols are of a standard that compares well with others manufactured elsewhere.

However, few Chinese pistols have been of original design, and among the many designs copied over the years, the old Mauser C/96 'broomhandle', and in particular its Model 712 variant (more usually known as the 'Schnellfeuer' in the West), was much favoured, to the extent that tens of thousands were imported from Germany during the 1920s and '30s. Once in China, they were directly copied in detail by local industry. At one time it was quite the thing for every Chinese senior officer to have a bodyguard armed with an imported or locally-made copy of a Model 712, and many small workshops churned out their own particular versions of the Mauser original to meet an avid demand. The seeming affection for the imposing Model 712 was little shared in other parts of the world, but for good reason the Chinese had a great respect for its extremely high rate of fire. The Model 712 came into the machine-pistol category, i.e. it was a hand weapon that could produce fully automatic fire at one press of the trigger (they are also sometimes referred to as machine carbines).

While the high fire rate did make the Model 712 a weapon to respect at close quarters, it was also extremely difficult to control. As soon as the trigger was pressed, a single burst of fire could empty the magazine, and the resultant violent recoil forces would rapidly force the barrel upwards, to waste most of the shots away from the target. However, the Chinese developed a technique of simply turning the pistol on its side so that, when fired on automatic, the pistol produced a horizontal and fearsome fan of fire that could clear a room.

The Chinese affection for the old Mauser pistol remains to this day. Some of the old pre-war examples may still be encountered on mainland China, and such is the local respect for the basic design that it is still in production, albeit in a much amended form.

The producers are the mighty China North Industries Corporation, usually known as NORINCO, who are now the main Communist Chinese armaments concern. Among their wide-ranging weapons output, which ranges from tanks and artillery to ammunition and land mines, they produce a Mauser C/96 derivative known as the Automatic Pistol 7.62 mm Type 80. Despite its cleaned-up and smoothed-off outlines, including a revised butt shape, it can still be recognised as a Mauser. The Type 80 is a machine pistol that can produce bursts of fire at a cyclic rate of 60 rounds a minute (much slower than the old Model 712, which could churn out up to 900 rounds a minute) and to accommodate this output, two sizes of vertical box magazine are available, one holding 10 rounds, the other 20. The mechanism is, for a pistol, rather complicated, being based on an internal reciprocating bolt allied to an external hammer. If required, single shot fire can be selected, but the main attraction for the Chinese is the automatic fire capability.

In order to keep the pistol under some sort of control while firing on automatic, the old Mausers used to have a wooden holster that could be fixed on to the pistol butt to produce a form of machine carbine. The Type 80 carries over this principle, but instead of a solid holster the Type 80 uses a clip-on telescopic butt with a rudimentary butt stock. The carbine notion is even taken one stage further on the Type 80, by the addition of a short knife bayonet, making the Type 80 one of the few pistols ever intended to accommodate such an accessory.

Other changes made by NORINCO to the basic Mauser design include the slight tilting forward of the magazine housing. This introduces the cartridge to the feed mechanism at a more sympathetic angle than was originally the case, and so the feed

The Chinese Type 80 automatic pistol, clearly showing its Mauser ancestry.

overall is now even more reliable. The alterations to the butt outline have already been mentioned, but they must certainly improve the handling of the weapon - the old Mauser 'broomhandle' was not an easy butt to grip with comfort. It also seems certain that many of the old time-consuming manufacturing techniques involving hand machining and finishing have given way to more modern production methods - the magazine housing appears to utilize metal stampings.

It is likely that the Type 80 is used by the Chinese armed forces, and it has been offered for export, but few have yet to make their way outside China. Despite the age of its origins, the Type 80 should find some takers, for one of the main assets of the Mauser pistols has always been the ammunition employed. The original Mauser C/96s used the 7.63 x 25 mm cartridge which, in its time, was one of the most powerful and accurate available, so powerful in fact that for many years the Mauser C/96 pistol was one of the most favoured weapons utilized by political and professional assassins. The 7.62 x 25 mm Tokarev cartridge, known in China as the Type 51, is virtually identical to the Mauser original and therefore it makes the Type 80 a weapon to respect. The Chinese claim that the Type 80 has an effective range extending up to 150 metres (no doubt with the butt in use) and while not every user will obtain good results at such a range, it still extends the combat range of the Type 80 beyond many of its more modern contemporaries.

TYPE 67

Nation of origin: People's Republic of China
Ammunition: 7.65 x 17 mm
Operation: blowback or single shot
Weight: 1.02 kg
Length: 225 mm
Length of barrel: 89 mm
Magazine capacity: 9 rounds
Muzzle velocity: 181 m/s

By its very nature, the pistol is an ideal assassination weapon. It is lethal when used correctly, small, easy to conceal and quick to point and fire, so it is not surprising to learn that the pistol has long been the preferred weapon of the undercover killer and political assassin. The pistol does, however, have one inherent drawback that usually presents no particular problem, but quite often can. That drawback is the loud report produced by the pistol as it fires. A killer who wishes to draw no attention to his (or her) presence would not want to use such a noisy weapon, but the killing efficiency of the pistol is such that it often has to remain the preferred weapon. Under such circumstances a silencer has to be fitted to the pistol involved.

The term 'silencer' when applied to any firearm is something of a misnomer. Even the most efficient silencer applied to the muzzle of a pistol or other such weapon will serve only to muffle the firing report, and some degree of sound will still be produced. The best that can usually happen is that the silencer masks the firing report to such an extent that the resultant sound is unrecognizable as a shot being fired. Silencers also have the advantage that they can obscure any indication of the direction from where a muffled firing sound was produced. Some small-arms authorities prefer to use the term 'moderator' rather than silencer, as a result.

In any case, pistol silencers tend to be large and bulky things that are usually rather inefficient. Even so, they have been used on many clandestine occasions. Pistols designed from the outset to be 'silenced' are still rare, and few examples can be readily cited. There was the British Welrod pistol of the Second World War, but until the Chinese Type 64 silenced pistol appeared in the West, via some devious route, during the late 1960s there were few other similar weapons. The Type 64 was designed from the outset (exactly by whom within China is still not known) to be a true assassination weapon, with few operational roles to fulfil other than close-range silent killing. It was an odd 'one off' when it first appeared, and remained so until its stable mate, the Type 67, appeared a few years after.

To take the Type 67 as the more modern example, the Chinese silenced pistols have much to attract those with an interest in firearms. While it visually resembles a conventional pistol in many ways, the Type 67 reveals its intent by the large tube that surrounds the short barrel. This conceals a silencer (or moderator) system that extends forward of the muzzle, which is thus concealed well within the silencer housing. As the bullet leaves the muzzle, some of the propellant gases are allowed to expand within an enclosed chamber that contains a series of wire mesh baffles over a perforated sleeve. The bullet has to leave the weapon through a series of rubber discs that contain the bulk of the propellant gases, and so the greater part of the sound is absorbed inside the weapon and only a slight report can be detected from even a close distance, and virtually none from the sides or rear.

The sound produced by the Type 67 (and earlier Type 64) is further reduced by using a low power cartridge that is unique to these two pistols. It is a rimless 7.65 x 17 mm cartridge that cannot be used in any other weapon. Being low-powered, it largely avoids the high-pitched supersonic firing report of most conventional rounds, but the low power is a trade-off in penetration terms. The low power means that for effective employment the pistol has to be used at what are virtually point-blank ranges, but that is apparently deemed acceptable for an assassination weapon. That the short range is accepted is marked by the provision of only the most rudimentary of fore and rear sights.

To keep down the mechanical sounds of the weapon slide reciprocation and other mechanical happenings, both the Type 64 and Type 67 can use two methods of operation. For really silent operation it is possible to feed a round into the chamber, and a rotating bolt is then pushed home manually using the slide until lugs on the bolt ensure that the weapon is safely locked for the instant of firing. After the round is fired, the slide is retracted manually to eject the spent cartridge case and to feed a new round as the slide is pushed forward again. However, it is possible for the mechanism to operate semi-automatically using a simple blowback mechanism by moving a selector bar. In this mode the slide movement and feed produce some operating noise.

The earlier Type 64 differs from the Type 67 mainly in having a much bulkier housing for the silencer system. It is also heavier (at 1.81 kg) and less well balanced to handle, being somewhat muzzle heavy.

It has been mentioned that the Type 64 and Type 67 are assassination weapons, but it is conceiveable that they could have a more viable military role. Special forces often need to remove enemy sentries or other unfortunates without drawing attention to their presence, and silenced pistols could be used for this purpose. That was certainly the role envisaged for the British Welrod which was used by Commando and similar units until 1945. The Welrod was withdrawn soon after that date, for it became only too apparent that assassination weapons are double-edged devices. Once they fall into the wrong hands they can be used just as effectively against their perpetrators as by them, and for this reason other similar weapons are not widely distributed. Thus the Chinese silenced pistols remain just about the only examples of their type in service today - that is unless the Soviet Spetsnaz troops have something similar. The only other known weapon in this category is the seldom-encountered North Korean Type 64 silenced pistol (which is based on the old Browning Model 1900) and that was probably produced to foot the same bill as the Chinese Type 64 and Type 67.

VZOR 75 AND 85

Nation of origin: Czechoslovakia
Ammunition: 9 x 19 mm
Operation: short recoil
Weight: empty, 1 kg
Length: 203 mm
Length of barrel: 120 mm
Magazine capacity: 15 rounds
Muzzle velocity: approx. 390 m/s

Czechoslovakia has long been a large scale producer of weaponry of all kinds, even when the nation was part of the old pre-Great War Austro-Hungarian Empire. During the interwar years, Czech small arms designers devised many innovative weapons

The Czech vzor 85, the updated version of the vzor 75.

that were to influence numerous other small arms designs that appeared elsewhere, but after 1945 the nation found itself a member of what was to become the Warsaw Pact.

Unlike many of the other states that come under the remit of the Soviet Union-dominated Warsaw Pact, the Czech nation has continued to plough its own furrow and produce its own indigenous weapon designs. While a degree of weapon commonality with the rest of the Warsaw Pact nations has had to be accepted, the Czechs have been able to retain a certain amount of independence and have continued to produce their own weapons, not only for their own use but for export to many other nations elsewhere. Pistols have been part of their output, but for years prior to 1975, none were produced for export. The Czech armed forces are still armed with the Czech-designed and produced 7.62 mm vzor 52 (vzor means model) or the 7.65 mm vzor 50, both very sound and reliable weapons, but of only limited attraction to overseas buyers in the crowded small arms market.

The Czechs thus missed out on the pistol export scene to a large degree during the late 1950s and early 1960s. This loss was more than offset by export sales of other weapons, but the absence of an attractive pistol in the Czech arms sales catalogue was often felt. In 1975 that was put right by the appearance of the vzor 75.

The vzor 75 has been produced in only one calibre, the widely-used 9 mm Parabellum. That alone means that it cannot be issued to the Czech armed forces, for the Warsaw pact does not utilize the 9 mm calibre (they use the Soviet 7.62 x 25 mm Tokarev round, while the Czech armed forces also use a 7.65 mm pistol cartridge) so all sales efforts for the vzor 75 had to be made with an eye to exports. The Czechs have been remarkably successful in this difficult field, for the vzor 75 has many sales advantages, not the least of which is its relatively low price.

The vzor 75 was value engineered from the start. It had to be sold with a price tag that would attract buyers but the relatively low price involved could not mean a loss in quality. The opposite has proved to be the case, for the vzor 75 is one of the best pistols that the Czechs have ever produced. In design terms, it utilizes many of the best points taken from many other pistols, and introduces a few good points all of its own.

As it is meant to fire the relatively powerful 9 mm Parabellum cartridge, the blowback system was deemed insufficiently reliable, so the short recoil system was used instead. With this system, the barrel remains locked to the slide as it moves backwards after firing for sufficient time to allow the chamber internal pressures to fall to a safe level before the locking system is opened and the slide can move further to the rear for the eject/feed and recocking sequence to commence. The feed system involves a 15-round box magazine with the rounds stacked in a double-row pattern to conserve space and keep the butt dimensions to a manageable level. The safety mechanisms involved mean that an extra round can be carried safely in the chamber, making 16 rounds ready for use if required. The firing pin is kept well back from the cartridge in the chamber until the firing sequence is definitely initiated, and even dropping the pistol onto its muzzle will not result in an unwanted firing. To fire the pistol when a round is already in the chamber, there is no need to pull the slide to the rear. The external hammer is cocked by pulling the trigger for the first shot (once the safety catch has been removed).

The value engineering factor of the vzor 75 is largely achieved by using die castings for the slide and main frame. These are relatively cheap to produce and require only a minimum of machining before assembly, yet are quite adequate to withstand the stresses imposed upon them. As would be expected, the barrel is high quality steel, as are several other critical components.

Overall, the balance and 'feel' of the vzor 75 are first class, and have resulted in many export sales gained in the face of tough opposition, most of them made to the police forces of many nations. The customer has the option of walnut or plastic butt grips and can select either fixed sights, or a rear sight with a degree of lateral adjustment. Despite the weight of the weapon it is easy to hold and can deliver fire with accuracy up to the usual combat pistol ranges.

The qualities of the vzor 75 have been carried over to the more recent vzor 85. This is basically the vzor 75 (which remains in full-scale production) with a few enhancements to maintain its position in the market place. Some modifications have been introduced to the internal workings, but they are slight and the biggest change has been made to the manual safety catch and slide stop. On the vzor 75 these are located on the left-hand side of the pistol, but the vzor 85 has been revised to allow them to be fitted on either side and thus make the pistol more attractive to left-handed firers. Some other slight changes have been introduced on the vzor 85, but overall it retains the many attractive features of the earlier vzor 75.

To return to the vzor 75, it is licence produced in Switzerland by the Industrial Technology & Machines AG (ITM) of Solothurn. They have used the vzor 75 more as a starting point for their AT-84S, which is immediately recognizable as a vzor 75, but the Swiss have lavished their usual craftsmanship on the original and overall it is a much more refined product. The Swiss have introduced a new super high-quality barrel and some slight alterations to the safety mechanism. ITM have been successful in their sales efforts, to the extent that batches of the AT-84S have been sold to the Hong Kong Police and to some Australian police and security forces. ITM have also carried out a redesign of the Czech original to produce the AT-84P, which is smaller and lighter overall. A version of the AT-84 to fire the .41 Action Express cartridge is expected to appear in the near future - it might already have appeared by the time these words are read.

Any up-to-date account of the vzor 75 has to add a sour note to what would otherwise be the story of a good all-round pistol. The Indian government purchased 50,000 vzor 75 pistols direct from Czechoslovakia to equip the Indian Border Security Force and the Central Reserve Police Force. When the first pistols arrived they were deemed unsatisfactory, but for what precise reason is uncertain. The end result is that certain Indian ministers and military officers are having legal proceedings taken against them. The outcome of the case should be interesting.

SKORPION

Nation of origin: Czechoslovakia
Ammunition: 7.65 x 17 mm
Operation: blowback
Weight: empty, 1.59 kg
Length: butt retracted, 269 mm
Length of barrel: 112 mm
Magazine capacity: 10 or 20 rounds
Muzzle velocity: 317 m/s
Cyclic rate of fire: 840 rpm

The Skorpion is another weapon that falls into the category of machine pistol, i.e. it can deliver fully automatic fire. It was developed during the late 1950s and entered service with the Czech armed forces during 1961, hence the official designation of vzor 61. With the Czech military, the Skorpion is issued to personnel who by the nature of their duties cannot carry conventional weapons such as rifles or sub-machine guns, but who require a more effective weapon than a conventional pistol. Into this bracket fall armoured vehicle crews, signallers carrying backpack radio equipment, and so on. The Skorpion allows such personnel to defend themselves out to a useful combat radius (claimed to be up to 200 metres) and armoured vehicle crews can use the weapon against close-in tank-killer infantry squads operating inside the radius of the vehicle's self-defence weapons.

Where the Skorpion differs from other machine pistols is the ammunition employed. The vzor 61 Skorpion fires the 7.65 x 17 mm cartridge, the European version of the American .32 ACP. This is a relatively low-powered cartridge, so the Skorpion is able to make use of the simple blowback operating principle with the breech block operating against two return springs. The problem for the Czech designers was that, even with such a low powered cartridge as the 7.65 x 17 mm, the intertia of the breech block involved in a weapon the size of the Skorpion is such that, if left uncontrolled, the cyclic rate of fire on automatic would be far too high (it could rise to well over 1,000 rounds a minute) for the firer to control the weapon. They decided to include a fire rate reducer device in the pistol, and this enables the Skorpion to fire at a cyclic rate of about 840 rounds a minute.

The fire rate reducer is a combination of components in the

butt and at the rear of the square-sectioned receiver. As the breech block is blown to the rear it engages on a spring-loaded hook located at the end of the receiver and is prevented from being pushed back under return spring pressure towards the chamber. At the same time the breech block drives a spring-loaded plunger down into the butt where a system of weights and springs alters its speed of travel so that, as the spring-loaded plunger starts to rise again, it does so at a much slower rate. It is this spring-loaded plunger that releases the breech block from the hook on which it was held and allows the next round to be fed, chambered and fired. The Skorpion does not resemble other automatic pistols in having a slide, for the breech block reciprocates inside the receiver. The weapon is cocked by pulling back a domed cocking button on the left-hand side of the

The Czech Skorpion machine pistol with the wire butt folded. Note the curved box magazine and the button on the side of the receiver; the latter is the cocking device.

receiver; the button is connected to the breech block.

The fire rate reduction device in the butt means that the magazine has to be located in front of the trigger guard. The magazine is slightly curved and may hold 10 or 20 rounds, with the operational emphasis being placed on the 20-round magazine; when firing on automatic it does not take long to fire off all available rounds. Needless to day, the barrel movement when firing bursts is still lively, and firing the pistol on automatic with one hand is not recommended when accuracy is required, no matter how impressive it may appear visually. To enable more control, the Skorpion is fitted with a rudimentary wire butt that folds up and over the receiver in a neat fashion when the pistol is stowed in its holster. Firing the Skorpion one-handed on single shot is stated to be easy and accurate. One small point must be remembered when firing the Skorpion: the ejector slot is on top of the receiver, so that if the weapon is fired from

The Skorpion in its intended combat mode being used from an armoured vehicle.

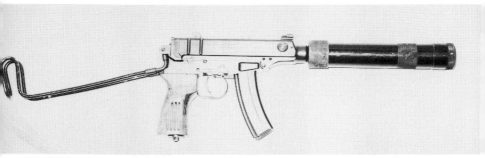

A Skorpion fitted with a silencer (moderator) and with the wire butt extended.

around waist level and close to the body, it is possible for ejected cases to hit the firer in the face.

The Skorpion was issued to the Czech armed forces and has been widely exported, especially to Africa where the weapon is much favoured by the personal bodyguards of heads of state and other senior officials. In order to make the weapon more attractive to potential buyers, the Skorpion was produced in several calibres. The first was the vzor 63, which fires the American 0.38 Auto round. Then came the vzor 64 firing the 9 x 18 mm Makarov cartridge, now widely used by Warsaw Pact and Soviet-influenced nations. Finally there was the vzor 68 which fires the ubiquitous 9 x 19 mm Parabellum round. All Czech versions of the Skorpion are now out of production, but a licence-produced 7.65 mm version is still produced in Yugoslavia for issue to the Yugoslav armed forces and for possible export sales; it is known as the Model 61(j).

Despite its odd hybrid nature, for by being a machine pistol the weapon is neither a good pistol nor a good sub-machine gun, the Skorpion may be widely encountered. It is still in front-line service with the Czech armed forces and, as has been mentioned, may be found in use with nations such as Ghana, Mozambique, Uganda and Angola. However, the main impact of the Skorpion these days is likely to be in the hands of various forms of 'freedom fighter' who have discovered that the Skorpion is a remarkably effective weapon at short ranges and in enclosed areas. Skorpions have been noted during television newsreel coverage of the fighting in Lebanon.

It was no doubt with terrorist/freedom fighter employment in

mind that a silenced (or moderated) version of the Skorpion was developed. With this version there was no pretence at a highly efficient or special silencer system, for the Skorpion silencer is simply a long tube containing a number of rubber baffles and a muzzle plug through which the bullet has to travel after leaving the muzzle. The silencer tube screws on to a thread incised into a special barrel extension, while the baffles simply damp down the sound of a cartridge firing. No attempt is made to reduce the sound of breech block movement. It would appear that the silenced model was intended for single-shot use only. When in position, the silencer prevents the wire butt folding down over the muzzle. The silenced version of the Skorpion is rarely seen, and not many appear to have been produced.

WALTHER PP and PPK

Model	PP		PPK
Nation of origin:	Germany		Germany
Ammunition:	7.65 x 11mm	or	9 x 17 mm
Operation:	blowback		blowback
Weight:	0.682 kg		0.568 kg
Length:	173 mm		155 mm
Length of barrel:	99 mm		86 mm
Magazine capacity:	8 rounds		7 rounds
Muzzle velocity: (7.65 mm)	290 m/s		280 m/s

The world of modern combat pistols is beset by the fact that many of the pistol designs still in widespread use today date back many years. The fact that they appear in a book of this nature can be put down to the fact that when they first appeared, they were in many ways ahead of their time, and their continued production can only be attributed to the overall excellence of their original design. This is particularly true of the Walther PP and PPK pistols.

The first Walther PP (PP - Polizei Pistole) appeared as long ago as 1929. 1929 was not a particularly good year for pistol sales, for not only was the world recession then in full swing, but Germany was still recovering from the Great War. Military sales of new pistols were at an all-time low. However, the designers at the Walther factory, then at Zella Mehlis in what is now East Germany, detected a possible requirement for a pistol to be used by police forces to replace the various bulky revolvers that were then in widespread use. The result was the PP.

It was an immediate success. All over Europe, police forces were glad to get rid of their many and various revolvers and pistols that, in many cases, dated back to the turn of the century. They were immediately attracted by the smooth lines and excellent handling qualities of the Walther PP. Before long, large numbers were pouring off the Walther production lines to fire either the 7.65 x 21 mm Parabellum cartridge, long favoured by many Central European police forces, or the 9 x 17 mm Short cartridge (not to be confused with the more powerful 9 mm Parabellum) based on the American .380 Auto cartridge.

The Walther PP design was based on that of an earlier Walther pistol, the Model 8. This pistol, only one of a long line of Walther pistols dating back to 1908, had been produced in the early 1920s to fire the then-obsolescent 6.35 mm cartridge, and by enlarging the overall dimensions and introducing an external hammer, the PP was produced. The PP is a simple design mechanically, using the straightforward blowback operating principle, with the overall lines being sleek and smooth. User firing comfort was indulged to the extent that an optional magazine extension spur was provided under the butt to provide an even better grip for large-handed policemen. One refinement that was, and still is, much appreciated and which went on to become a virtual Walther trademark was the introduction of a small signal pin that protrudes from the rear of the slide when the chamber is loaded. Thus the user can tell the loaded state of the pistol at a touch. Safety was not ignored in the design, for the firing pin is locked by the safety catch to allow the hammer to be lowered safely, even when a round is in the chamber, and the pistol will not fire unless the slide is fully forward and a definite trigger pressure is applied.

The PP was intended for use as a belt holster pistol, but as not all policemen wear uniforms all the time, it was decided to produce a smaller vesion of the PP for use as a pocket or concealed

A Walther PP in 7.65 mm calibre.

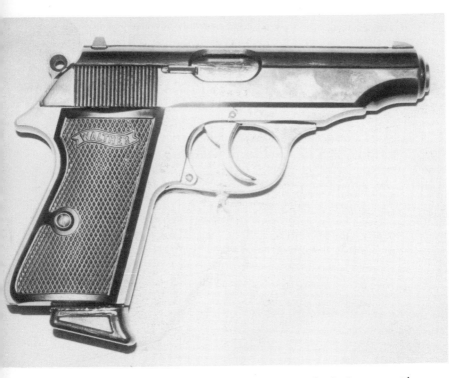

The Walther PPK — note the magazine extension under the butt to provide a more comfortable firing grip.

weapon. This emerged in 1931 as the PPK, or Polizei Pistole Kurz, (*Kurz* meaning short). The PPK is smaller overall, with a shorter barrel and a reduced magazine capacity (by one round) but it is basically the same pistol as the PP and has enjoyed all the success of its larger counterpart.

During the Second World War, huge numbers of PP and PPK pistols were produced for the German armed forces, especially for the Luftwaffe, but the war ended with the Walther factory inside what had become East Germany. Walther resumed production in a factory at Ulm-am-Donau and, as soon as permitted, continued to produce the PP and PPK for a market that is still eager for them. The pistol production locations proliferated. For a while the East Germans produced a direct copy of the PP, and both PPs and PPKs were produced in Turkey, Hungary and France (by Manhurin). The Czech vzor 50 was closely modelled on the PP, as was the Polish P-64, and many other pistols have

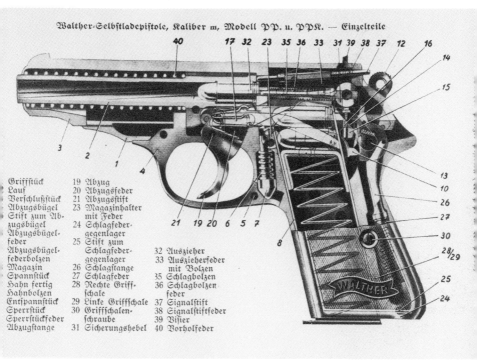

Walther-Selbstladepistole, Kaliber m, Modell PP. u. PPK. — Einzelteile

Griffstück	19 Abzug	
Lauf	20 Abzugsfeder	
Verschlußstück	21 Abzugsstift	
Abzugsbügel	23 Magazinhalter	
Stift zum Ab-	mit Feder	
zugsbügel	24 Schlagfeder-	
Abzugsbügel-	gegenlager	
feder	25 Stift zum	
Abzugsbügel-	Schlagfeder-	32 Auszieher
federbolzen	gegenlager	33 Auszieherfeder
Magazin	26 Schlagstange	mit Bolzen
Spannstück	27 Schlagfeder	35 Schlagbolzen
Hahn fertig	28 Rechte Griff-	36 Schlagbolzen-
Hahnbolzen	schale	feder
Entspannstück	29 Linke Griffschale	37 Signalstift
Sperrstück	30 Griffschalen-	38 Signalstiftfeder
Sperrstückfeder	schraube	39 Visier
Abzugstange	31 Sicherungshebel	40 Vorholfeder

Extract from a war-time manual for the Walther PP showing the workings of the pistol.

signs of PP and PPK influence. Many have detected the influence of the PP in the Soviet PM (q.v.).

Production at Ulm continues apace, with no signs of demand slackening. Both pistols continue to be carried by police forces all around the world, and various armed forces also use them. One example of the latter is the British Army. They issue PPs to off-duty Ulster Defence Regiment soldiers (and others) who might be at risk from terrorist attentions, and to undercover personnel operating in plain clothes. To the British Army the PP is the 7.65 mm Pistol Automatic Walther Type PP XL47E1.

Over the years the basic PP and PPK have remained unchanged, and what modifications have been introduced have been minor. It is possible to obtain examples with dural slides (to reduce weight slightly), sights with luminous spots for easier aiming under poor lighting conditions, and many examples dating from the war years have some refinements such as the usually excellent finish, and the signal button on the slide, missing. These days a large proportion of production is for civilian shooting enthusiasts who continue to value the PP and PPK highly, but both types are still purchased for use by their original intended market, namely police forces.

By the way, it should not be forgotten that James Bond's favoured pistol was the Walther PPK.

Modern pistols from around the world

Above and below *The FN Mark 3 Hi-Power pistol with all the latest innovations such as an ambidextrous safety catch and revised grips for improved firer comfort.*

Above *The cocking lever of the Heckler & Koch P7 M13 shows up prominently in this photograph.*

Below *Right-hand side of the Heckler & Koch P7 M13.*

Above *Cross-section of a Heckler & Koch P7.*

Below *The Uzi pistol in use demonstrating the overall large dimensions of the weapon.*

Above *A Pistolet Makarova, complete with its holster holding a spare magazine and a cleaning rod.*

Above left *The 9 mm Beretta 92F, the pistol selected to become the US Armed Forces new M9.*

Below left *A 9 mm SIG P225 at full recoil.*

Left *Cross-section of a SIG P226, showing the main components.*

Below *Field stripping a 7.62 mm Pistolet Makarova.*

The quick draw is still very much an aspect of pistol-handling skills. Here a trained pistol handler demonstrates a quick draw sequence using a Smith & Wesson Model 459.

Above *Not covered in the text is the South African Z88, which is in use by the South African security forces. This locally-designed and produced 9mm Parabellum pistol was first shown in October 1988 and appears to have Beretta design influences, but with some features all of its own. The Z88 uses a 15-round magazine and weighs under 1 kg empty. The action is the usualy double-action with an open hammer. The picture shows two views of a finished Z88 pistol, plus 2 stages of the machining involved in manufacturing the main body and grip. The Z88 is manufactured by the Lyttleton Engineering Works, located not far from Pretoria.*

Below *The 9 mm Smith & Wesson Model 39, the first pistol in a sequence that led to the model 645.*

WALTHER P1

Nation of origin: Federal Republic of Germany
Ammunition; 9 x 19 mm
Operation: locked breech
Weight: empty, 0.772 kg
Length: 218 mm
Length of barrel: 124 mm
Magazine capacity: 8 rounds
Muzzle velocity: 350 m/s

The section devoted to the Walther PP and PPK should provide an indication of the importance of the Carl Walther Waffenfabrik concern on the European pistol scene. Their design experience was such that when the German armed forces began to expand and rearm, following Hitler's coming to power, they were asked to submit a pistol design to replace the ageing Luger Pistole

A Walther PI in the neatly-gloved hand of a German military policeman.

'08 (P'08) as the standard German service pistol.

Walther used all their experience to come up with a design, originally known as the 'Armee Pistole', or AP. This appeared in 1937 and was a new design with a locked breech operating system to accommodate the power of the 9 mm Parabellum cartridge that was carried over from the Luger P'08. The German authorities were impressed, but requested some changes, including the addition of an external hammer. That resulted in the 'Heeres Pistole' (service pistol, or HP). This the Army liked but again, some slight changes to make mass production easier were requested. The Pistole 38, or P38, then entered production during 1938.

The P38 remained in production until 1945 and proved itself to be a superlative service weapon. It was so good that once the new West German Bundeswehr was formed during the 1950s, the P38 was requested as their standard service pistol once again. Thus in 1957 the P38 was put back into production by Walther at their Ulm-am-Donau factory, but by then it was known as the Pistole 1, or P1.

The P1 is largely unchanged from the earlier P38. The main modification is the introduction of a light alloy (dural) slide in place of the earlier steel component, and some slight internal alterations have been made. The P1 can be readily identified by its protruding barrel and the chubby slide with a pronounced cutaway on the top. The double-action trigger mechanism enables the weapon to be cocked and fired by a single pull of the trigger (provided a round is in the chamber). The hammer strikes an internal firing pin and at the instant of firing the barrel is locked to the slide by a ramp. The recoil forces then cause the barrel and slide to move backwards locked together, until the barrel is prevented from moving further by a fixed stop; the slide continues to travel rearwards. By then, the internal chamber pressures will have fallen to a safe level and the rest of the ejection, feed and hammer cocking sequence can continue ready for the next shot.

Some of the safeties used in the earlier PP have been carried over to the P1. When the safety catch is applied, the firing pin is securely locked and cannot move. This means that the external hammer can be lowered safely when a round is in the chamber (this will happen automatically as the safety catch is actuated), although this should not be tried on old P38s, especially those

A Walther P1 at the ready.

produced during the war years when manufacturing standards were lower. The signal pin on the slide rear face, which protrudes slightly when a round is in the chamber, is another PP carry-over.

For combat pistol users, the main attribute of the Walther P1 is that the high standard of construction and quality of the materials employed mean the weapon is incredibly tough and will remain capable of firing reliably, even under the worst possible service conditions. Like any other weapon, it performs best when regular maintenance is lavished upon it, but under operational conditions this is not always possible. Here the P1 excels, for it will continue to function even when covered in all manner of dirt and debris, and with ammunition that might be of doubtful quality.

It is also an excellent pistol to handle and fire. It has smooth lines with few protruberances to snag on clothing or equipment, and once in the hand it demostrates its excellent balance and aiming qualities. If the P1 does have a drawback, it is that the eight-round capacity of the box magazine is now much less than that of many other pistols in service elsewhere. The ammunition in the magazine remains as potent as it was when it was first devised during the early 1900s, as the 9 mm Parabellum is still a prodigious man-stopper.

The P1 is in service with the West German armed forces, and with many West German police forces. Export sales have been made to the armed forces of nations as disparate as Portugal, Norway, Chad and Chile, and to many police forces. To meet demands made by some police forces, a special version with a barrel shortened to only 70 mm was developed, and at one time was evocatively designated the P38K. A 7.65 x 21 mm Parabellum version was in production at one time, and there has even been a .22 version, for sales to target shooters. Numbers of P38s from the war years may still be encountered in police, arm-

The Walther P 38 K, clearly showing its attenuated barrel.

A war-time-production Walther P 38 with a standard of finish far inferior to that of the modern P1. The P1 differs also in having a light alloy slide in place of the steel slide used on the P 38.

ed forces and freedom fighter armouries all around the world but, as has been indicated above, the standard of finish and manufacture of some of these older weapons is nowhere near as good as those lavished on recent production examples. Service P1s are usually recognizable by their overall matt black plating, while examples for the commercial market are often produced in a pronounced glossy blue finish; commercial models are known as the P4.

One small comment on the weapon that the P1/P38 was meant to replace: the Luger Pistole '08 is once more in production, this time by the Mauser-Werke at Obendorf, but the customers are no longer military. Modern production Lugers are sold to a wide spectrum of well-heeled pistol buffs and collectors.

WALTHER P88

Nation of origin: Federal Republic of Germany
Ammunition: 9 x 19 mm
Operation: locked breech
Weight: empty, 0.9 kg
Length: 187 mm
Length of barrel: 102 mm
Magazine capacity: 15 rounds
Muzzle velocity: approx 350 m/s

The pistol is a lethal weapon that is meant to kill. What the pistol is not meant to kill is the person using it, or persons he (or she) does not wish to kill. This rather obvious statement is made necessary by the fact that, over the years since it was first devised, the pistol has quite possibly killed as many (or more) 'friends' as it has 'enemies'. Many of these unwanted casualties have been inflicted by the pistol's inherent characteristics, including its short length, which makes it all too easy to point unintentionally in the wrong direction, and very often an over-light firing action. Unwanted shots can also result from hammers snagging on clothing or vegetation, and many pistols have a nasty propensity to go off when jarred, or dropped even a short distance.

All these inherent danger points have tended to make the pistol a weapon subject to much scrutiny. Many military and police authorities abhor them, and put up with pistols only in the absence of any better form of light and portable personal weapon. But if there is one single design trend that can be discerned over the last two or so decades, it is the move to producing ultra-safe pistols.

Many of the factors that make pistols unsafe have been built into pistol designs that date from times when there was little or no customer demand for inherent pistol safety. In the past, many military authorities scarcely bothered with the need to specify safety mechanisms, other than requesting the provision of a basic safety catch. What extra safeties were incorporated into pistols were usually placed there by thoughtful designers, without any prompting from customers. Over the last 20 years or so, that has changed to the point where military and police customers have begun to insist on really safe pistols, or at least pistols that are as safe as can be devised. The one thing that

The handsome lines of the Walther P88.

cannot be changed is the short barrel length of the pistol. That still means that pistols are as easy to point unwittingly in the wrong direction as they ever were. Only common sense and self discipline will prevent accidents continuing to happen on that score.

That still leaves mechanical safeties. One obvious safety is the locking system itself. When one is dealing with cartridges as powerful as the 9 mm Parabellum, simple blowback mechanisms must be considered as inherently unsafe. Some more definite locking system is required. Carl Walther Waffenfabrik had for long used a positive (and very effective) locking system on their P38 and P1 pistols, but when they introduced their P88 pistol they had decided to go one better, introducing a slight variation of the locking system used on the older Colt-Browning automatic pistols.

With this system, the slide and barrel are locked together by lugs on the barrel fitting into recesses on the slide at the instant of firing, when the internal chamber pressures are at their highest and therefore at their most dangerous to the firer and to the fabric of the pistol itself. The slide and barrel move to the rear locked together, until a cam on the barrel strikes a lug that tilts the barrel slightly and enables the two components to unlock, leaving the slide free to move to the rear by itself. By that time the chamber pressures will be at a safe level, as the bullet will have left the muzzle. This system means that the old top cut-away slide of the P1 cannot be used, so the Walther P88 has taken on a more conventional appearance and externally resembles many other pistols. However, its smooth and positive outlines make the P88 one of the most handsome automatic pistols on the market today.

The resemblance to other designs is superficial, for many differences from other pistols are present. One is on the safety arrangement for the firing pin. On too many pistol designs, any time the firing pin is struck by the hammer, no matter how unintentionally or lightly, the result is a cartridge discharged. Various ingenious mechanical means have been introduced to prevent this happening, but on the P88 it is accomplished by keeping the firing pin depressed at all times other than when the trigger is definitely pressed. Should the hammer fall or move on to the firing pin recess, it will not hit the firing pin unless the trigger has been positively pulled and the firing pin has been pushed up to receive the hammer pressure and fire the round in the chamber. As the trigger is released the firing pin is once again lowered out of the way.

This simple-sounding arrangement is not very easily transferred into practice, for the method of raising and lowering the firing pin is rather complex, but it works to the extent that the user can carry the P88 with a round loaded in the chamber, happy in the fairly certain knowledge that many of the usual unwanted shot-producing causes (dropping, snagging the hammer on clothing, etc) are avoided. To fire the pistol, all that is necessary is squeezing the trigger to cock the hammer and allow it to fall on the intentionally-raised firing pin.

If the hammer is cocked and no further firing is required, it is possible to lower the hammer again safely by using a de-cocking lever which is present on both sides of the receiver to accommodate right- and left-handed users. This lever also doubles as a slide release to allow the slide to move forward and close again after a magazine has been reinserted into the pistol following the emptying of a previous one. (As the magazine empties, the slide is automatically held open to demonstrate the need for more ammunition; this happens on most pistol designs.) This should not have to be carried out too often under combat situations, for the P88 box magazine holds 15 rounds. A further indication of the care taken in the design of the P88 can be seen by noting that a magazine release catch is provided on both sides of the receiver, close to the trigger, and that the front edge of the trigger guard is provided with a squared-off exterior outline to enable it to be grasped easily with the widely adopted two-handed firing grip. Another design detail is that the foot of the box magazine protrudes slightly from the end of the butt, to allow it to be grasped easily for removal.

The Walther P88 is a fairly recent product, and it has yet to make a significant break through into the pistol market, but many armed and police forces will no doubt be examining its many attributes with great interest. It was an early entrant in the US Army XM9 contest, but was withdrawn during the competition, no doubt to rectify some technical shortcomings that have by now been corrected.

HECKLER & KOCH P9S

Nation of origin: Federal Republic of Germany
Ammunition: 9 x 19 mm
Operation: roller-delayed blowback
Weight: empty, 0.88 kg
Length: 192 mm
Length of barrel: 102 mm
Magazine capacity: 9 rounds
Muzzle velocity: approx 350 m/s

Ever since the 1950s, when West German armaments manufacturers were permitted to produce weapons again, the firm of Heckler & Koch has been one of the most successful and innovative of all German manufacturers. Working from the old Mauser factory at Obendorf-Neckar, Heckler & Koch made their name with the G3 series of assault rifles that utilize a novel roller locking system developed during the latter years of the Second World War. The roller locking system has the advantage of being simple, easy to manufacture and very reliable, so reliable

The Heckler & Koch P9S pistol - compare with the near identical P9.

*The Heckler & Koch P9 pistol, the
first of the Heckler & Koch pistols to
use the roller locking system (Heckler
& Koch).*

that when Heckler & Koch decided to enter the military pistol
market it was not long before the roller system was carried over
into an automatic pistol known as the P9.

The Heckler & Koch P9 pistol was developed into the P9S,
which was intended from the outset to be a military pistol. As
with so many other military pistols, it was designed to use the
9 x 19 mm Parabellum cartridge, but some were modified to fire
the 7.65 x 21 mm Parabellum round, and for the American
market a special version to fire the 0.45 ACP (Automatic Colt
Pistol) has been produced.

The roller locking system makes use of a two-part breech
block. One part is a bolt head which carries two rollers. The second part is a heavier bolt body which, when held forward under
return spring pressure, forces the rollers on the bolt head out-
wards, to latch into recesses in a barrel extension. As the pistol
is fired, the resultant recoil forces attempt to move the bolt head
and body to the rear but the rollers, being located in the barrel
extension recesses, will not move until the forces on the bolt
head have overcome the inertia of the bolt body and the forces
of the return spring which tend to keep the bolt assembly forward. The end result is that the bolt assembly will not move, and
remains locked in place until the rollers have been forced in-
wards against all the resisting forces. The residual pressure in the

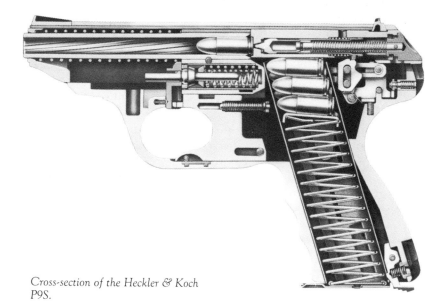

Cross-section of the Heckler & Koch P9S.

chamber will then drive the bolt assembly to the rear to carry out the relocking and reloading procedures. At the end of its rearward travel, motion of the bolt assembly is arrested by a plastic buffer.

This may sound rather complicated, but the roller locking system is basically a simple mechanism that is very positive and safe. It has been used without problems on tens of thousands of G3-series rifles and similar weapons, and it works very well on the P9S.

The locking system apart, the P9S has some other unusual features. One must be the form of the rifling used, which does not assume the usual groove and lands pattern, but instead employs a polygonal cross section. This is not unique to the P9S, for polygonal rifling has been used on some other pistols (such as the Austrian Steyr GB, now out of production) and was pioneered on the early Whitworth field artillery pieces of the 1860s. The advantages of the polygonal system are claimed to be that the polygonal outline offers less resistance to a projectile passing through it, and the bullet is subjected to less deformation in the process. Experts argue long into the night upon such topics, but for the ordinary user the main advantage is that it is far easier to clean than the more conventional rifling grooves, and resists fouling much more readily.

Unlike the pistols mentioned in this book so far, the P9S does not have an external hammer. This is claimed to be an extra safety point, for although most military users like to be able to tell the state of a pistol at a glance (such as an obviously cocked hammer), the hammer is usually prone to knocks and unwanted changes of state in tight situations. On the P9S, the hammer is internal and entirely concealed, but the state of the pistol can be readily checked by the provision of a pin which protrudes from the rear of the slide. This can be checked at a glance, or by touch in the dark. The presence of a round in the chamber is denoted by the spent cartridge extractor, which stands proud in the ejector slot when a round is chambered. In this way the inherent safety of an internal hammer can be provided, without losing the visual and tactile indications of the pistol's loaded or unloaded condition.

If the hammer is cocked and no firing is required, the hammer can be lowered safely using an external cocking lever. The safety must be engaged before this is carried out, and once the cocking lever has been actuated, the mechanism is cleared by pulling the trigger to release the hammer safely. The cocking lever is then allowed to rise to its normal position, and the trigger is released.

The P9S is primarily a military pistol, but it has proved to be an excellent target-shooting weapon. For competitive target shooting, the P9S can be fitted with a barrel 140 mm long, in place of the usual component which is 102 mm long. The longer barrel can be fitted with a muzzle attachment which adds weight, to make the pistol better balanced for accurate shooting. To make the P9S even more of a competition shooting weapon it is possible to fit an adjustable trigger stop device that can be used to vary the trigger pressure to suit individual users more closely. The rear sights are also adjustable, and for the really keen pistol shot, anatomically-moulded butt grips can be fitted.

One feature that will appeal to many military users is that the P9S lacks the usual blued finish so often applied to pistols, and is instead covered with a thin coating of a hard-wearing plastic film. This adds to the pistol's smooth outline, but is not so smooth that it will slip from fingers when wet, and is a definite factor in keeping corrosion and wear at bay. The normal firing grip is very positive and secure, and two-handed grip firers are provided for by the now widely-used reverse curve at the front of the trigger guard.

The P9S has been a definite success in sales terms, ever since it first appeared in 1975. Many have been sold to police and security forces all around the world, and it is still in production for the many pistol enthusiasts who like to own and fire superb examples of the pistol designer's art. One military user is the US Navy where SEAL (Sea Air Land) teams have obtained numbers of the P9S to conduct their special missions. By virtue of the special-forces use of the P9S with the SEAL teams, some have been fitted with silencers. Another military user is Greece.

HECKLER & KOCH P7 SERIES

Nation of origin: Federal Republic of Germany		
Model	M8	M13
Ammunition:	9 x 19 mm	9 x 19 mm
Operation:	delayed blowback	
Weight loaded:	0.95 kg	1.135 kg
Length:	171 mm	169 mm
Length of barrel:	105 mm	105 mm
Magazine capacity:	8 rounds	13 rounds
Muzzle velocity:	351 m/s	351 m/s

When Heckler & Koch developed the P9S (see previous entry), they were thinking in terms of a military pistol. When they developed the P7 series of pistols, they were thinking in terms of police pistols. Although armed and police forces both carry pistols, they can expect to use them in action in different ways and in differing circumstances. Military pistols have to undergo the rough and tumble of field operations, while most police pistols spend long periods of time carried in snug holsters and are rarely drawn in anger. When police pistols are drawn with intent, they have to work faultlessly but safely, or there will be all manner of problems, to say nothing of dead policemen.

Thus when Heckler & Koch produced the P7 they decided to make changes from the normal run of pistols. For a start they did away with the usual array of locking systems. Once again, the almost universal 9 x 19 mm Parabellum cartridge was chosen for the new pistol by the continuing demand. To deal with the recoil forces involved, the selected locking system turned out to be an unusual gas-operated delayed blowback system.

The P7 locking system was employed widely for the first time with the German 'last ditch' series of Second World War 'Volkspistole' of 1944 and 1945. As the round in the chamber is fired, some of the propellant gases are directed through a port close to the chamber into an enclosed chamber. The front part of the chamber is the face of a piston connected to the slide. As the recoil forces attempt to drive the slide and its integral breech block to the rear, the gases in the chamber are still expanding and exert pressure to keep the piston in place. By the time

Above *The World War 2 'Volkspistole', an unusual weapon designed for mass production during the latter stages of the war, and one of the first to employ the gas-operated delayed blowback operating system now used on the Heckler & Koch P7.*

Left *The range of Heckler & Koch pistols, from the top: 7.65 mm P7 K3; P7 PT8 firing plastic training ammunition (note the spot near the muzzle); 9 mm P7 M13; 9 mm P7 M8; 9 mm P9S Sport sporting target pistol; standard 9 mm P9S.*

the recoil forces overcome the internal chamber gas pressure, the bullet has departed from the muzzle and chamber pressures have fallen to a safe level, and the slide and breech block can then move to the rear. This gas-delayed blowback system is positive, simple and reliable, and has the advantage that some of the recoil forces produced on firing are absorbed by the gas pressure. There are also fewer parts to wear out or break.

The P7 locking system is unusual in itself, but it is allied to a rarely-employed cocking system. To fire the weapon, the chamber is loaded by pulling the slide to the rear in the usual way and allowing it to slide forward again. A round is chambered and as the firer grips the butt, his hand grip automatically depresses a contoured lever on the front of the grip to actuate the cocking mechanism. The pistol will remain cocked for as long as the firer's grip is maintained, and will fire when the trigger is pulled in the normal way. If the grip is released, the pistol will return to an uncocked state.

The grip device acts as the pistol's safety mechanism for the simple reason that no other device is required. The pistol is suitable for use without modification by right- and left-handed users, and again the system is simple and reliable. Overall reliability is further improved by the way the box magazine is angled. For good and consistent feed, automatic pistol box magazines should offer their cartridges to the breech block from a near vertical position. If this was carried to its logical conclusion, automatic pistol grips would be vertical as well, but that would make them awkward to grasp. Most modern pistols have angled grips for user comfort, ease of aiming and a firm grip, so most magazines have to be angled as well. On the P7 the butt is angled but wide, wide enough for the magazine to be almost vertical inside the butt, to improve the feed angle to an optimum for feed reliability.

Police forces have learned the hard way that most policemen are poor shots unless constant training is provided, so on the P7 aiming is made as easy as possible. The usual fore and rear sights are provided but the fore sight bears a prominent white dot and the rear sight has two more white dots, one each side of the rear sight notch. By placing all three dots side-by-side and in line with the target, aiming is made as rapid and easy as can be devised without recourse to far more complex methods. Aiming is assisted by the good balance of the weapon and the large and comfortable butt grip.

There are two main versions of the 9 mm P7. The P7 M8 has an 8-round magazine, while the P7 M13 holds 13 rounds. The P7 series does not end there. There is the smaller and lighter P7 K3 which does away with the gas delay system altogether and employs simple blowback instead, as it fires less powerful cartridges such as the 9 x 17 mm Short, 7.65 x 17 mm Browning or 0.22 rounds. The P7 K3 is intended for use as a staff officer or plain clothes police pistol, and retains the grip cocking device.

Then there is the P7 PT8. This is not intended to be a combat pistol, but a training pistol that can fire a special training round produced by Dynamit Nobel; the pistol is otherwise identical to a conventional P7. The training round was designed to enable useful pistol training to be carried out safely and relatively cheaply on short indoor or outdoor ranges, and the maximum range is only 125 metres. The cartridge fires a soft plastic bullet, is identical visually and dimensionally to the conventional 9 mm Parabellum round and is accurate at short ranges. It has been suggested that the training cartridge combined with the P7 PT8

The Heckler & Koch P7 M8 pistol — note the cocking lever in the front of the butt.

could have an operational role in locations such as in pressurized aircraft to counter hijacking or other criminal actions. Other similar operational scenarios could be possible.

A recent variant of the basic P7 about which little has yet been released is the P7 M45. This has been designed for the American market, chambered for the .45 ACP cartridge, and differs from the standard P7 in using oil instead of gas to produce the delayed blowback locking system. On the P7 M45 the internal piston operates in a cylinder filled with oil. As the recoil forces tend to push back the internal piston after firing, they attempt to compress the oil. As the oil is compressed, it is gradually circulated through a closed-loop system by a release valve in such a manner that the travel of the piston is hindered to the point where the recoil action is made smooth and far less violent than is possible using a conventional action. The entire recoil process is rather like that used in an artillery recoil system. At the time of writing, the P7 M45 had yet to be released on to the market, for the recoil system was still in its final stages of development.

It should be remembered that the P7 series pistols were intended as police pistols. While they have had considerable success in that sphere, including breaking through into the difficult American police force market, just as much success has been achieved in the military market. Special forces units all around the world have taken to the P7 with considerable gusto, and many now use it as their main side arm, while more conventional armed forces have also ordered the type. One example that can be quoted is Greece where the local govenment arms production organization (Hellenic Arms Industry SA) have taken out a licence production agreement to produce the P7 for the Greek armed forces and local exports - they call 'their' examples the EP7.

UZI PISTOL

Nation of origin: Israel
Ammunition: 9 x 19 mm
Operation: blowback
Weight: loaded, 2.14 kg
Length: 240 mm
Length of barrel: 115 mm
Magazine capacity: 20 rounds
Muzzle velocity: approx 350 m/s

The Israeli Uzi pistol is certainly one of the more unusual-looking pistols to be found anywhere today, for although it is meant to be a semi-automatic pistol for use as a personal side arm, it has obvious affinities with the Uzi sub-machine gun from which it was developed. For the Israelis, the Uzi sub-machine gun has become something of a symbol of their past success in fighting off threats to their national existence, and so successful is the Uzi that it has been sold widely to many armed and security forces all around the world, including the West German armed forces.

Bearing in mind that Israel is a small nation with limited production and human resources, it was a natural process that the basic Uzi should be worked upon to produce new weapon designs. One of the first of these was the Mini-Uzi which was a scaled down version of the standard Uzi, followed by the even smaller Micro-Uzi. Both are 9 mm Parabellum models intended for use by special forces or security guards. These designs remained sub-machine guns, despite their small dimensions (although some pedants would prefer to call them machine pistols), and it was not until the Uzi Pistol appeared during the mid-1980s that the scaling-down process produced a weapon that could be placed in the true pistol category. Even so, the Uzi Pistol is still a bulky and heavy design, compared to most of its contemporaries.

The Uzi pistol was designed to meet a requirement for a weapon to act as a self-defence measure for Israeli civilians, although no definite announcement appears to have been made. The possibility of guerrilla attack on Israeli settlers in locations such as the West Bank and the northern border areas of Israel has been present for many years. Attacks have materialized in

many forms over the years, and large numbers of Israeli settlers
understandably feel themselves constantly under threat. They
have accordingly called for arms with which to defend
themselves, rather than having to rely upon the often hard-
pressed regular security forces. Some of the settlers' demands
have been met by the issuing of all manner of small arms, or by
the settlers arming themselves, but since most of the weapons involved had to be imported, the Israeli government attempted to
produce something locally to conserve limited foreign exchange
funds. The Uzi Pistol has been one result.

Despite its bulk and seemingly awkward appearance, the Uzi
Pistol is well suited to the civilian defence role. One important
point is that it is immediately familiar to most potential users.
Nearly every adult Israeli, male and female, has handled and
fired the Uzi sub-machine gun during their periods of national
service, so handling the Uzi Pistol should present no problems.
The Uzi Pistol can also be produced within Israel using existing
machinery and other resources, and it makes few demands on
expensive raw materials since most of the construction uses sim-

*The boxy outline of the 9 mm Uzi
pistol.*

ple sheet steel or other 'non-strategic' metals and plastics. Manufacture is straightforward, involving a minimum of costly machining processes.

The Uzi Pistol is immensely strong. The weight and bulk of the weapon means that it is capable of taking all manner of knocks and still keep on working. Thus it is an ideal weapon for carrying around in the dust, mud and rain of border settlements, rattling about in vehicles such as tractors, being left around in a state of 'benign neglect' and exposed to all manner of weather conditions for long periods. It is also an ideal weapon to be carried on the long and repetitive guard duties that many outlying settlements have to conduct. One further point in the Uzi Pistol's favour is that it fires the readily-available 9 mm Parabellum cartridge, already in large-scale production inside Israel. Maintenance is no great problem, since there are only seven parts involved in field stripping.

The Uzi Pistol is not a machine pistol: the trigger mechanism will operate on semi-automatic only. There is no receiver slide, and cocking is carried out by pulling back a breech block lever on top of the receiver, There is no breech locking mechanism other than the blowback system that relies upon the weight and mass of the large breech block involved. As with the Uzi sub-machine gun, the breech block extends forward and around the forward part of the barrel, allowing the box magazine to feed vertically upwards through the butt. Firing the Uzi Pistol is no doubt a lively procedure, for the barrel is short, but by most accounts a good proportion of the recoil forces are absorbed by the weight of the weapon itself. One definite asset that the Uzi Pistol possesses is its large magazine capacity. In any local defence situation, the knowledge that there are 20 rounds in the pistol ready to fire could provide a very reassuring morale booster. The usual safety catch is coupled with a grip safety device on the rear of the butt grip; unless the butt is securely gripped, depressing the grip safety, the pistol will not fire.

The Uzi Pistol is in production, but to date there are no indications that any have been supplied to the Israeli settlers for whom the weapon was intended. Instead the pistols are now advertised in pistol enthusiast magazines for sale as sporting pistols, which covers a wide swathe of territory. Considering the form of construction used with the Uzi Pistol, its price appears high and the market would appear at first sight to be rather limited.

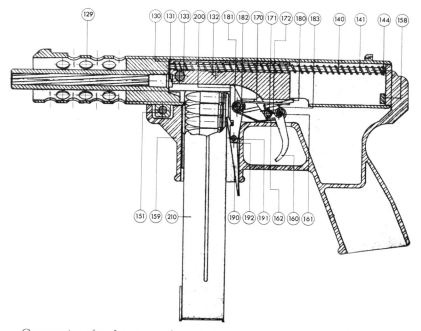

Cross section of an Intratec machine pistol, an American weapon similar in design approach to the Uzi pistol; the numbers refer to spare part serial numbers.

There are also certain to be sales restrictions placed on the Uzi Pistol in many countries, for it falls into a weapon bracket known as the heavy pistol. These are now being viewed with considerable suspicion by many police forces. Weapons such as the Uzi Pistol may not be as powerful as some of the more potent Magnum-firing pistols but they do have large magazine capacities and provide the user with a considerable amount of potential firepower. This can only add to the headaches of law enforcement agencies of many countries. Other examples of the heavy pistol include the odd-looking Goncz pistols (from the United States) that are easily turned into carbines by the addition of a butt, and the Intratec series of pistols, again from the United States. These are what can only be described as miniature semi-automatic sub-machine guns, complete with magazine capacities of up to 36 rounds and optional screw-on barrel extensions. The very thought of such weapons in criminal or terrorist hands should be enough to make even the most ardent pistol enthusiast understand why so many people advocate weapon ownership restrictions.

DESERT EAGLE

Nation of origin: Israel
Ammunition: .357 Magnum or .44 Magnum
Operation: rotating bolt
Weight: empty, steel frame, 1.701 kg
Length: with 152 mm barrel, 225 mm
Length of barrel: 152, 203, 254 or 356 mm (see text)
Magazine capacity: .357 Magnum, 9 rounds; .44 Magnum, 7 rounds

When one encounters the Desert Eagle pistol, one enters the world of pocket artillery, for the Desert Eagle is currently one of the most powerful automatic pistols available anywhere in the world. Strictly speaking, the Desert Eagle is not really a combat pistol, but it is inevitable that some will find their way into military or police hands and thus find a use far removed from the competition benches for which the Desert Eagle was originally intended.

The Desert Eagle had its origins in the United States when the first examples were produced by a company known as M.R.I. Limited of Minneapolis. The pistol was developed to meet a demand from the gun buffs who are attracted primarily by having the most powerful or largest of anything. There is a considerable interest in producing and firing powerful hand-loaded cartridges in the United States, and from this enthusiasm for producing something more powerful than that used by the other guy, grew the Magnum cartridge concept. Quite simply this meant putting more than the usual amount of propellant charge into a cartridge to fire a heavy, often blunt-nosed, bullet with the resultant on-target effects being dreadfully effective and impressive (the 'Dirty Harry' syndrome). The main problem for pistol designers was that the Magnum rounds are too powerful for the orthodox breech mechanisms used by most automatic pistols. Almost all the pistols produced to fire Magnum ammunition had been revolvers until the Desert Eagle appeared. Revolver frames are simple, have few moving parts and can be built to be strong enough to take the firing stresses involved with Magnum cartridges.

It was not long before someone decided to produce a Magnum-firing automatic pistol. That someone was M.R.I. Limited, and at first the intended market was the sporting pistol buff. As so

This photograph of a Desert Eagle about to be fired clearly demonstrates the large overall dimensions of this pistol.

often happens with small arms innovations, design skills were not matched by marketing abilities, and eventually Desert Eagle production switched to Israel, where all manufacturing and marketing is carried out by Israel Military Industries (IMI).

In order to overcome the considerable chamber pressures inherent in Magnum rounds, the Desert Eagle uses a fixed barrel combined with a rotary breech locking system. This type of locking system is now widely used on assault rifles and other weapons, but to find it employed in a pistol is unusual. As a cartridge is chambered, a rotary lock on the face of the breech block engages in lugs around the chamber. As the cartridge is fired, a proportion of the propellant gases are tapped off through a gas port close to the chamber, and impinge upon a piston. The piston is driven to the rear and pushes two side arms which in turn operate a cam to turn the rotary breech block head and so unlock the breech. By that time, the chamber pressures will have fallen to a relatively safe level and the usual recocking and reloading sequences can proceed.

Safety has to be an important factor on a pistol as powerful as the Desert Eagle, and applying the ambidextrous safety catch not only locks the firing pin, but disconnects the trigger mechanism as well. The safety system is claimed to be efficient to the extent of preventing firing even when the pistol is accidentally dropped onto its hammer.

What is not immediately discernable with the Desert Eagle is its large overall scale and weight. It is a bit of a handful to tote around and this, coupled with the fearsome recoil forces produced by Magnum rounds, means that it is not a pistol to be handled by the novice. This alone has made some potential military and police users draw back from procuring the type. The noise, flash and recoil 'jump' are enough to make the raw recruit nervous about even handling the weapon, to the extent that only prolonged and careful training can make the Desert Eagle a viable service pistol. In the hands of a trained user the Desert Eagle is a fearsome weapon and a prodigious man-stopper, to the point where an adversary could not fail to be knocked over and disabled by the traumatic shock of even a non-lethal hit. This makes the Desert Eagle an attractive weapon to special forces and paramilitary police units where the necessary training is available. In the hands of a tyro, the Desert Eagle is inevitably

A trio of Desert Eagles. The example at the top has a stainless steel finish; the centre weapon is fitted with an optional long barrel and has a standard barrel just underneath; the bottom example is finished in a rather unusual camouflage scheme which would appear to be more emotive than practical.

quite a handful and a potential danger to all, but there could be situations where even the sight of a pistol the size of the Desert Eagle could be enough to make potential assailants think twice.

The Desert Eagle is produced in two forms; one chambered for 0.357 Magnum and the other for 0.44 Magnum. Both versions have identical external dimensions, but the magazine capacity is reduced from nine rounds to seven on the 0.44 model. Both versions can be produced with steel or aluminium frames. The standard barrel is 152.4 mm long, but to suit individual competition shooting requirements the standard barrel can be easily removed without recourse to tools and replaced by a barrel 203, 254 or 356 mm long. The longer barrel lengths are used for long range competition shooting in conjunction with optical (telescopic) sights that can be mounted on grooves in the barrel. This pistol can also accommodate a range of complex and adjustable 'iron' sights, and to take the individual competitor's requirements to full account it is possible to replace the entire rear assembly with an optical adjustable assembly.

All these refinements will be of little interest or utility for the combat pistol user. He will be concerned primarily with the combat shooting qualities of the Desert Eagle, and the pistol has many attractions. Apart from the distractions of its size and bulk, the Desert Eagle is extremely well made (it has to be to accommodate the firing stresses involved) and well balanced, and its projectile is dreadfully effective on target. The main problem is quite simply the handling of the weapon. Military and police small arms instructors already have quite enough to do to make recruits handle conventional pistols safely and sensibly. They often have to overcome inherent fears and poor aiming produced by the noise and recoil forces involved with lesser rounds. Exactly how they would teach trainees to handle the pocket artillery cartridge loads associated with the Desert Eagle is a considerable training challenge.

It would seem safe to assume that any military or police employment of the Desert Eagle will be confined to specialist users who have the time and facilities for the training involved, and the sense to use the pistol properly, and safely, if it ever has to be used operationally.

One item of late news is that there are rumours about a version of the Desert Eagle that will soon be produced to fire the .41 Action Express cartridge.

BERETTA 92F

(Data refers to Model 92F/M9)
Nation of origin: Italy
Ammunition: 9 x 19 mm
Operation: short recoil
Weight: loaded, 1.145 kg
Length: 217 mm
Length of barrel: 125 mm
Magazine capacity: 15 rounds
Muzzle velocity: approx 390 m/s

Beretta pistols have for long enjoyed an enviable reputation for all-round quality and for having superb shooting characteristics. They have also managed to maintain a distinctive appearance that marks them as Beretta products, despite the large number of models that have been developed over the years. When the Beretta Model 92 appeared in the mid-1970s it was immediately recognizable as a Beretta, even though it was much larger than the usual run of Beretta 'pocket pistols' that had done so much to establish the company name and reputation.

One of the main recognition points on Beretta pistols is the long cut-away section over the barrel, combined with a wrap-over guide close to the muzzle to carry the fore sight. This was

The basic Beretta Model 92 from which all the subsequent Model 92 variants have been derived.

The Beretta Model 92S, a pistol closely allied to the Model 92F.

carried over to the Model 92, as was the general aura of careful design and good lines. The Model 92 was a large pistol, as it had to fire the 9 mm Parabellum cartridge. Locking was achieved using the short recoil system.

The Model 92 was soon adopted by the Italian armed forces, where the 15-round capacity of the box magazine was much appreciated. Brazil was another satisfied customer. But the Model 92 was only the start of a series of pistol models to which new variants are apparently constantly being added. First to appear was the Model 92 S which had a modified safety. Then came the Model 92 SB which had several features to make it more suitable for left-handed users, and the safety mechanism was revised. This was followed by the Model 92 SB-C which was a scaled-down version of the Model 92 SB.

However we will concentrate on one particular variant of the Model 92 SB, the Model 92F. The Model 92F was developed specifically to meet a requirement issued by the United States Army to replace their venerable Colt M1911 series of pistols. These veterans had been in American service since 1911 and were well outdated if not just about worn out, many having been rebuilt using spare parts several times during their military careers. Over the years a virtual separate industry had grown to keep the massive numbers of M1911s supplied with spares, accessories and other services to the point where design

The 9 mm Beretta Model 92F, one of the most successful pistol designs of recent years.

developments elsewhere overtook the American pistol industry.

Although the fact was not immediately discernable under the welter of new pistol designs that constantly issued from American pistol manufacturers large and small, the big American names such as Colt and Smith & Wesson were gradually being left behind in all manner of pistol innovation such as inherent safeties, improved handling features, new materials and, perhaps the most important, new ammunition. While the 9 mm Parabellum cartridge could hardly be called new, it was virtually unknown within the United States other than from imports. American producers and users continued to select the trusted 0.45 ACP (Automatic Colt Pistol) cartridge used in the M1911. Almost every other military user elsewhere turned to the 9 mm Parabellum and the round became a NATO standard item. The American forces simply had to change, so the US Army issued a requirement for a new 9 mm pistol, the XM9, during the late 1970s. Their specification took account of all the improvements already built into many modern European pistols, and it caught American manufacturers on the hop.

Pistol development is a time-consuming business and it was too late when the Americans realized that their existing products could not easily meet the XM9 specifications. When the first 'shoot-off' competition took place, the result was that the contest was dominated by European manufacturers. However, none of the entrants was deemed successful. Many considered the contest to have been rigged to favour the American entries, but as none of them got through the selection process either, the result was yet another competition, held during 1984. Once again the Europeans dominated the proceedings, to the point where at the end of it all two European entrants were selected and one of them was finally adjudged the 'winner', apparently by being the least expensive product of the two.

The winner was the Beretta Model 92F, the variant of the Model 92 SB developed specifically for the US Army contest. It is now the M9 Pistol and is in production both in the United States and Italy to meet an initial production contract for 315,930 pistols at an initial cost of $53 million - that works out at $175 each, which is just over a quarter of the commercial price. The M9s will be delivered over a five-year period, with initial production being delivered direct from Italy. After an interim changeover period, all production will be carried out in the United States.

The old and the new; on the left is the old Colt .45 M1911 'Government Model', while on the right is the pistol that will replace it as the US Armed Forces' standard service pistol, the Beretta Model 92F, or M9 (US Army).

The M9 differs from the Model 92 SB in having a revised trigger guard outline plus an extended magazine butt to accommodate a two-handed grip, a lanyard ring at the base of the butt, a chromed barrel and revised grip plates. The pistol is finished with a film of a hard plastic-like material known as 'Bruniton' that reduces glare and resists wear.

It would be foolish to state that the American pistol industry has taken the award of the M9 contract to Beretta without demur. At the time of writing, there was still talk of legal action, contest reruns and a general air of discontent that a 'foreign' concern should take a contract that historically should have gone to an American company. But the Italians did get the contract and are sticking to it by opening a production line in the United States (at Accokeek, Maryland). Although their contract was won mainly on cost grounds over their Swiss competitors (SIG, with the P226 - q.v.), the award of the M9 contract has meant that many other potential Beretta users are making their way to the Beretta headquarters at Brescia to order the Model 92F, or something like it, for their own armed forces and other agencies.

They have plenty of models to choose from. There is now a Model 92F Compact, a Model 92 SB-C Type M, which is a revised version of the Model 92 SB-C, and various Model 92

The Beretta Model 92F Compact, a slightly revised version of the basic Model 92F.

The Beretta Model 99, a 7.65 mm
version of the Model 92SB-C, just
one of the many variants of the basic
Beretta Model 92.

derivatives chambered for the 7.65 x 21 mm Parabellum round.
But overall the most important model in numerical terms is the
Model 92F. If the Model 92F/M9 is good enough to meet the
stringent specifications and selection procedures of the
American armed forces, it should be good enough to meet just
about any military requirement.

Beretta have produced another winner.

BERETTA MODEL 93R

Nation of origin: Italy
Ammunition: 9 x 19 mm
Operation: short recoil
Weight: with 20-round magazine, 1.17 kg
Length: 240 mm
Length of barrel: 156 mm
Magazine capacity: 15 or 20 rounds
Muzzle velocity: 375 m/s
Cyclic fire rate: approx 1,100 rpm

The Beretta Model 93R falls into the category known as selective fire pistols. It is designed to be a hand-held weapon that can produce bursts of automatic fire, but strictly speaking it is not a machine pistol. This type of automatic weapon is a pistol that produces bursts of automatic fire to last for as long as the user keeps the trigger depressed, or until the ammunition supply runs dry, the latter being the more usual. Selective fire pistols produce limited bursts of fire only.

The latter point is important. Machine pistols have largely gone out of fashion, apart from anomalies such as the Czech Skorpion (q.v.) and the Chinese Type 80 (q.v.), for the simple reason that the bursts of fire produced are so high that the recoil forces of even low-powered pistol cartridges can rapidly built up until the weapon becomes virtually uncontrollable, leading to most of the shots in a burst being wasted away from the intended target. With selective fire weapons, the number of rounds in a burst is controlled by an internal counting device that will stop the shooting, even if the trigger remains depressed. On the Beretta 93R the number of rounds in a controlled burst is limited to three. After that number of rounds has been fired, the barrel will almost inevitably have been pushed of the target by the recoil. The Beretta 93R retains a single shot capability.

Very basically, the burst limitation device is a rotary cam with four faces. As the trigger is pulled, the cam rotates and each of the first three faces of the cam will allow the sear mechanism to release the firing mechanism to fire a round. As the cam rotates to its fourth face the firing mechanism is automatically disconnected, and no further firing is possible, even if the trigger is kept actuated. Only by releasing the trigger and pulling it once again

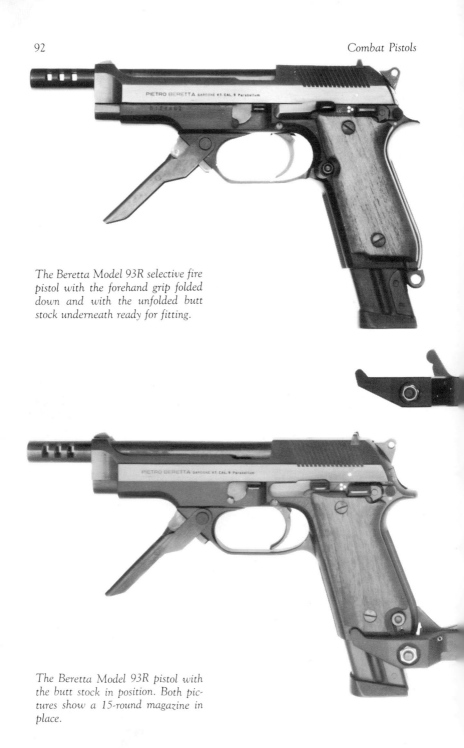

The Beretta Model 93R selective fire pistol with the forehand grip folded down and with the unfolded butt stock underneath ready for fitting.

The Beretta Model 93R pistol with the butt stock in position. Both pictures show a 15-round magazine in place.

will the rotary cam start turning again to control another three-round burst. The principle sounds fairly simple, but putting it into practice in a weapon as small as a hand gun is no easy matter. The development phase of the Model 93R was therefore somewhat protracted.

The burst limitation device is not the only measure used to keep the Beretta Model 93R under control when firing on full automatic. One unusual feature in a pistol of any nature is a muzzle brake, and the Model 93R has one with side-mounted ports to vent part of the muzzle blast away to the sides and keep some of the muzzle movement usually produced on burst firing under limited control. The device also acts as a useful muzzle flash hider for use during night operations.

Perhaps the most unusual control method is the form of foregrip device introduced on the Model 93R. This has been closely examined by many other pistol designers and it will be surprising if it does not reappear on other similar weapons at

some future date. The double-hand firing grip mentioned elsewhere in this book is now widely used, as it allows the firer to take a much more deliberate and steady aim than is possible by holding the pistol with just one hand. However, even the double hand grip has a limited capability to control burst fire, so the Beretta designers have altered the grip layout somewhat by pro-

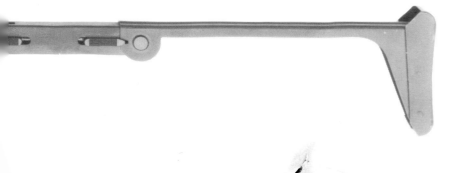

viding a compact folding foregrip. This is hinged on the forward-part of the trigger guard, and when not in use folds up under the receiver. When folded down it can be grasped by the hand not gripping the butt, with the thumb inserted into the forward part of the elongated trigger guard. The resultant hold is much firmer and enables the firer to maintain a better control of the weapon as it tries to move about during firing. Another advantage bestowed by the enlarged trigger guard is that it enables the weapon to be fired when wearing cold weather or NBC protection gloves.

Beretta recommend that the forward grip device is employed when the pistol is firing bursts. It is further recommended that use is made of a folding skeleton butt stock accessory that can be clipped on to the base of the butt to provide even more firing stability. When the butt stock is fitted, firing should be carried out from the shoulder, which also makes for more accurate aiming.

When the Model 93R is fired in the burst mode it is difficult to tell the three firing reports apart, for the cyclic rate of fire is about 1,100 rounds a minute. In many tight situations such a high fire rate would be invaluable, but only if the point of aim remains somewhere near its intended target. That can only be achieved in such a small automatic weapon by limiting the number of shots in the bursts. Ammunition supply is also a problem with automatic fire. The Beretta 93R can use two sizes of box magazine, the standard 15-round version or a longer 20-round component.

The basic frame and magazine used for the Model 93R were taken from the Model 92 (see previous entry) and the basic short recoil operating method was carried over as well. By the time the Beretta technicians had incorporated the various features of the Model 93R, little else other than the general outline of the earlier model remained. The Model 93R fire selection lever is on the left-hand side of the receiver with the three-round burst position graphically denoted by three white dots. Maintenance and field stripping of the weapon are simple and straightforward, but one part of the pistol that is not recommended for the attentions of field personnel is the burst control mechanism. The components involved were the source of a number of technical improvements during the development phases of the Model 93R and still require the care of a trained armourer should they ever cause trouble.

Overall, the Model 93R is a bulky weapon for a pistol but it does have a definite operational role. Many special forces personnel have to keep both hands free for various tasks and yet still have to carry an automatic fire weapon to fight their way out of tight situations or inflict the maximum firepower impact on a hapless target. Here the Model 93R could be an asset, for it can be carried in a somewhat oversized but easily portable holster arrangement and remain ready for use in an instant while at all other times the carrier/user is able to keep both hands free for climbing, swimming, or whatever else special forces personnel get up to while at work. Not surprisingly, the Model 93R is already in service with the special forces units of the Italian armed forces, and it has attracted the attention of similar units from several other nations.

STAR MODEL 30 M and 30 PK

Model	Model 30 M	Model 30 PK
Nation of origin: Spain		
Ammunition:	9 x 19 mm	9 x 19 mm
Operation:	short recoil	short recoil
Weight empty:	1.14 kg	0.86 kg
Length:	205 mm	193 mm
Length of barrel:	110 mm	98 mm
Magazine capacity:	15 rounds	15 rounds
Muzzle velocity:	340-380 m/s	340-380 m/s

At one time, the Spanish pistol industry had a terrible name. All manner of inferior revolvers and automatic pistols were once produced, often in factories that were little better than backstreet workshops. Most of them were shoddily manufactured from inferior materials. Nearly all of them were direct unlicenced copies of existing pistol designs, and their only sales advantage was that they were cheap and readily available. Not surprisingly, Spanish pistols were looked upon with suspicion by the discerning pistol user and at one time the term 'Spanish pistol' was one of derision.

The 9 mm Astra Model A-80, a contemporary of the Star Model 30 M; this is a typical example of modern Spanish pistol design and is available chambered for several types and calibres of pistol cartridge.

That was unfortunate, for among all the cheapjack merchants were some companies whose quality of output was second to none. In the long run, these companies prevailed when all the others were swept away by the backlash of customer dissatisfaction and lack of sales that had resulted by the end of the 1950s. Although there are a few second-rate Spanish pistols still to be found in the more disreputable corners of the small arms market (mostly of the 'Saturday night special' variety), the Spanish pistol scene is today dominated by two companies who have built up an excellent international reputation.

The two companies are Star Bonifacio Echeverria SA of Eibar and Astra-Unceta y Cia SA of Guernica (usually known simply as Astra). These two concerns continue to produce first-class pistols that are eagerly sought after by pistol enthusiasts, and the range of models produced by both companies is large. We will dwell upon only one basic Star-produced model, and use that as an indication of the standard of modern Spanish pistols generally. The corresponding Astra products are just as good.

The Star pistols involved are the Model 30 M and Model 30 PK. They are both basically the same pistol, with the Model 30M having a conventional steel frame while the Model 30 PK has a light alloy frame and is slightly smaller and lighter overall. Developed from the earlier Model 28, the two Model 30 pistols are fairly conventional designs, but have one unusual feature in that the slide has its runners sliding along inside the main frame, instead of along the exterior as is usually the case. This serves to keep the slide movement well supported throughout its travel and reduces friction and wear over a long period.

Both versions of the Model 30 use the short recoil operating principle. This widely-used system is one in which the barrel moves to the rear under the impetus of the recoil forces produced on firing, along with the slide to which it is locked by a rib on the barrel locating into a recess on the slide. After a short length of travel the lug on the barrel is knocked out of its recess by the barrel tilting as its movement is arrested by an oval-shaped cam. The slide is left free to complete its travel. This breech-locking method is simple, safe and mechanically reliable. .

The two pistols each have four separate safety mechanisms. One is the usual prevention of firing once the 15-round box magazine has been removed, but this feature can be overriden if it is deemed undesirable. There is also a locking safety whereby the pistol will not fire unless the slide is fully home and a round is securely located in the chamber. Then there is an ambidextrous safety catch that, when applied, keeps the firing pin out of line with the hammer. What is unusual with this safety catch is that the hammer and double action trigger mechanism are still free to operate. The trigger can be pulled to raise and release the hammer when there could be a cartridge in the chamber, so some users may not find this particular safety arrangement very reassuring. Finally there is the usual detent on the hammer that will engage the hammer in the half-cock position, should the hammer either slip from wet fingers when being cocked, or should it knock against a hard surface.

One extra safety factor is a chambered round indicator. When a round is located in the chamber and the slide is forward, the front end of the extractor is raised and reveals a red dot on its upper surface to provide a tactile and visual indication of a loaded pistol.

The Model 30 pistols have excellent shooting characteristics

The 9 mm Astra Model A-90, an updated version of the Astra Model A-80, also available chambered for the .45 ACP cartridge.

and the manufacturers claim they can be used accurately up to a range of 50 metres. At that range the 9 mm Parabellum projectile is able to penetrate 100 mm of pine boards, so the effect on living targets can well be imagined. Firing at such ranges is aided by the now commonplace reverse arc on the forward portion of the trigger guard, and the butt is well-shaped and angled. The rear sight is adjustable laterally and the top surface of the receiver is grooved to prevent reflected glare affecting accurate aiming.

Field stripping for regular maintenance is simple. More involved stripping can be accomplished with the aid of a cleaning rod supplied with the pistol - the removed firing pin and other components can be used to assist some of the stripping and assembly operations.

The Model 30 M is one of the standard Spanish armed forces service pistols, along with the Astra A-80. It is also used by the various Spanish police forces, and export sales have been made to nations such as Peru and Kenya.

The Star Model 30 M and Model 30 PK are typical examples of the modern Spanish pistol industry, and are sound and ser-

viceable weapons. The Astra pistols are no less worthy of con-
sideration; between them, Star and Astra have placed the
Spanish pistol industry on to a much higher level than that
which it once occupied.

SIG P225 and P226

(Data for P226)
Nation of origin: Switzerland
Ammunition: 9 x 19 mm
Operation: short recoil
Weight: empty, 0.75 kg
Length: 196 mm
Length of barrel: 112 mm
Magazine capacity: 15 rounds
Muzzle velocity: 350 m/s

With the SIG automatic pistols, one is dealing with superlatives; they are the Rolls-Royces of the pistol world. The only term that can be used to describe SIG pistols is superb, not only in aspects of handling and reliability, but in sheer quality of workmanship. So good is the quality of the SIG output from their main plant at Neuhausen Rhine Falls that one acquaintance of the author's owns a brand new SIG P225 that he is determined never to fire in case the appearance is somehow spoiled. He knows there is no danger of that happening, but just wants to keep owning a beautiful pistol!

The latest round of SIG pistol models commenced with the in-

The SIG P220, the base model for the later P225 and P226. This pistol is used by the Swiss Army as the 9 mm Pistole 75.

*The SIG P225; the P226 entered for
the US Army trials is essentially
similar (SIG).*

troduction of the P220 during the early 1970s. This pistol was the
base model for the later P225 and P226. All three models use the
short recoil operating principle with the breech being unlocked
after a short barrel and slide recoil movement, when a short lug
under the barrel hits a fixed post. The firing mechanism of the P220
is unusual, for after loading by inserting the box magazine (the P220
magazine holds nine rounds) the slide is allowed to slide forward,
leaving the hammer cocked. If the pistol is not to be fired the hammer is lowered by using a hammer decocking lever just above the
trigger on the left-hand side of the receiver. Once the hammer is
lowered, a series of safety mechanisms ensure that the pistol cannot be fired without a deliberate pull on the trigger. At all other
times the hammer is blocked from striking the firing pin. Even if
the pistol is dropped, it will not fire. There is no safety catch in
the usual sense, and all that is required to fire the pistol from its

safe state is a direct trigger pull, allowing a short into-action time comparable to that of a revolver. The pistol can be fired using either a double- or single-action. Close tolerances on all moving parts ensure good seals to keep out mud, dirt and other debris that could cause malfunctions.

The P220 is the standard Swiss service pistol and has been sold to some other nations, including Denmark and Nigeria. Well over 100,000 are in service and the pistol has also been produced to fire 7.65 x 21 mm Parabellum, 0.45 ACP (Automatic Colt Pistol, for the American market) and .380 Super. One factor that has restricted sales somewhat is that the overall excellence of the pistol and its workmanship means that it is very expensive. At one time the cost of a SIG pistol in the United States was the equivalent of at least four examples of any other comparable pistol.

The cost factor did not prevent SIG from producing the P225. It is basically a P220 with a light alloy frame and yet more safety factors built in. The overall dimensions have been reduced and the magazine capacity is reduced to eight rounds. These slight alterations have improved the balance of the weapon slightly and make it an even better pistol to handle and fire. To reduce training ammunition costs, it is possible to fit a .22 conversion unit to the P225 but the more recent training ammunition unit firing Dynamit Nobel 9 mm plastic ammunition is certain to be widely used to provide more realistic and safe training at short ranges. There is a choice of sights available, including high-contrast sights that show up well under poor lighting conditions. If required, the normal plastic butt grip plates can be replaced by wooden components.

The P225 has enjoyed its share of sales and is used by many Swiss and West German police forces, and some have been sold to the Swedish armed forces.

When the US Army issued their specifications for their XM9 pistol during the late 1970s, SIG decided that their product should be able to meet all the specified requirements. In 1980 SIG introduced the P226 specifically for the US Army competition. To provide an example of the quality of the P226, SIG have proudly announced that it is the best pistol they have ever produced. The P220 and P225 were used as the starting point, to the extent that over 80 per cent of P226 components come from those two models. The main alteration on the P226 involves the magazine capacity, which has been nearly doubled to 15 rounds, and the butt has been

Above *The SIG P230 is a blow back design that is not allied to the P220 series. It is intended for use as a police pistol and is available in a range of calibres.*

Right *The full range of SIG pistols: from the top, P226; P225; P220; P210; bottom pistol is the P230.*

enlarged accordingly. Another modification is the provision of an ambidextrous magazine catch.

The P226 went right through the US Army's demanding procurement, testing and 'shoot-off' procedures with flying colours, to the point where it finally emerged alongside the Beretta 92F (q.v.) as one of the two 'winners' of the long and involved XM9 selection contest. Many of the personnel directly involved in the M9 contest declared that they preferred the P226 over the Beretta product, but in test terms there was little to choose between the two. In the end the contract was awarded to Beretta for, as always, the excellence of the SIG P226 had to be paid for and this was reflected in the price. The M9 contract may have gone to Beretta, but one immediate result was an improvement in P225 sales within the United States - the good word soon got around.

Those American customers were not alone. The West German armed forces were so impressed that they have procured numbers of P226 pistols to serve alongside their P1s (q.v.) as their P6, and Singapore has been another customer. Perhaps these purchasers have noted one thing that has been overlooked elsewhere: the superlative workmanship and quality of materials employed in the SIG pistols means that they will last for years and years. Examination of hard-used examples of older models of SIG pistols will reveal very little wear, while perusal of log books (where kept) will usually show that very few, if any, components have broken or have needed replacing. Should any part replacement be required, all components of each model are interchangeable across that model range. Thus the initial high procurement costs can be more than offset by the reduced life cycle costs.

The combat shooter will worry little about such economic niceties. He will be far more concerned with the excellence of workmanship inherent in the SIG pistols, the definite reassurance provided by the positive and reliable safety mechanism and the smooth and sure trigger action. He will be further impressed by the balance and accuracy of the weapon, to the extent that he will have few doubts that he is indeed handling the Rolls-Royce of automatic pistols.

PISTOLET MAKAROVA

Nation of origin: USSR
Ammunition: 9 x 18 mm
Operation: blowback
Weight: empty, 0.663 kg
Length: 160 mm
Length of barrel: 91 mm
Magazine capacity: 8 rounds
Muzzle velocity: approx. 315 m/s

Three things mark most Soviet pistol designs: mass production, robust construction and longevity. The mass production aspect is simply explained by the sheer numerical size of the Soviet armed forces. A strictly adhered-to policy of standardization means that when a new weapon design is approved for service, it must rapidly become a standard issue for as large a proportion of the Soviet military population as possible, to keep down logistic and other unwanted burdens to an absolute minimum. That means that only one type of pistol ammunition needs to be produced,

7.62 mm Pistolet Makarova.

Above Right-hand side of a 7.62 mm Pistolet Makarova; note that this example lacks the usual star on the pistol grips.

Below The 7.62 mm TT-33 Tokarev automatic pistol that was replaced in front line Soviet use by the PM; huge numbers of TT-33 pistols are still in service all around the world.

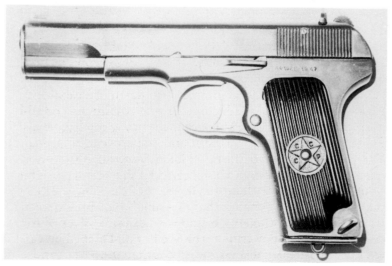

stockpiled and supplied to the troops, as well as only one set of pistol spare parts, unified training, and so on. The only way that a pistol can meet these massive requirements is to be produced by the tens of thousands, and the PM has indeed been churned out in the desired numbers.

Mass production was particularly important during the early 1950s when a new pistol cartridge was adopted by the Soviet Union, which in practice meant for all the armed forces within the Warsaw Pact. For decades, the standard Soviet pistol had been the TT-33 Tokarev firing the 7.62 x 25 mm Type P cartridge. By the 1950s both were seen as being, at best, obsolescent and over-due for replacement. The result was the then-new 9 x 18 mm Makarov cartridge and two new pistols, but before leaving the TT -33 behind it should be mentioned that it is still widely used, both inside and outside the Soviet Union (Soviet military quartermasters rarely throw anything away). The TT-33 is still produced and of-fered for export sales by Communist China (as the Type 54) and Yugoslavia (as the Model 57).

One of the two new Soviet pistols was the PM, and the other the Stechkin APS. The Stechkin APS can be covered briefly: it was little larger than a conventional pistol, yet had a facility to produce fully automatic fire. As with all such weapons is was dif-ficult to control when producing such fire, and to add to its list of bad points it was a complex weapon and expensive to produce. It soon passed from production and apart from limited Soviet arm-ed forces use it is now encountered only in odd corners of the world and in the hands of terrorist-type organizations.

That leaves the Makarov PM (PM - Pistolet Makarova) to depict the second aspect of Soviet pistols, namely robust construction. Experience has demonstrated to the military authorities in the Soviet Union that any weapon they use has to be capable of withstanding the worst possible operational conditions and still keep on working. Thus the PM is well made, using good materials, and the overall design is kept as basic and simple as can be devised.

With the introduction of the new Makarov cartridge, the Soviet designers deliberately devised a pistol cartridge that was as powerful as could be produced without having to introduce breech lock-ing mechanisms more complex than the simple blowback system. Thus the 9 x 18 mm Makarov round is an example of a ballistic trade-off. It is not as powerful as the 9 x 19 mm Parabellum car-tridge, but has better combat characteristics than the next cartridge

The 9 mm Stechkin APS machine pistol. complete with its wooden holster that doubles as a butt stock.

down the pistol hierarchy, the 9 x 17 mm short, widely used in Browning pistol models produced in the 1920s and 1930s.

The employment of a blowback locking mechanism means that moving parts can be kept to a minimum. There are then fewer parts to wear out, break or require maintenance. The blowback principle is simple to an extreme. Breech locking at the instant of firing is accomplished by using a breech block that is heavy enough for its inherent inertia to withstand the recoil forces produced as the pistol is fired. By the time the recoil forces are powerful enough to overcome the inertia of the breech block and its backing return spring, the bullet will have left the muzzle and chamber pressures start to fall rapidly, but by then the recoil forces will have done their work and the breech block is on its way rearwards. On its way it will extract and eject the spent cartridge case and come to rest against a buffer at the end of the receiver, recocking the firing mechanism in the process. The return spring (or springs) then starts to push the breech block back to its original position, chambering a fresh round as it travels, and we are back to the ready-to-fire position.

The rest of the PM is as basic and straightforward, for there are no frills on this design. Safety mechanisms are limited to the usual catch, slide safety, magazine removal safety and the imposition of a block between the hammer and firing pin when the safety catch is applied. These mechanisms are not as foolproof as some of the more complex devices employed elsewhere, but they are more than adequate.

The PM outwardly resembles the Walther PP (q.v.), but lacks

the fine finish and handling qualities of the West German pistol. By many accounts the butt angle makes the weapon rather awkward to aim comfortably, but that matters little to the Soviets, who are quite content to produce a weapon that will work when required and keep on working under all conditions. That brings us to the third point regarding Soviet pistols, the longevity; in many ways this third point involves the second.

All Soviet weapons are meant to last for a very long time. The previously-mentioned TT-33 Tokarev pistols can still be encountered in huge numbers, even though the last of the Soviet examples was produced in 1954, on production lines that started work in 1933. The first PM was produced during the early 1950s and it is still in production, not only in the Soviet Union but also in East Germany, where is it known as the Pistole M, but also in Communist China where it is known as the Type 59. The weapon seems set to become yet another long-term runner, and there is one further point of note. In the West, pistol manufacturers frequently make design changes to their high volume output in order to introduce various improvements and maybe cosmetic changes to keep their market buoyant. In the Soviet Union such commercial considerations do not apply, and the latest PM off the line will be found to be virtually identical to the first.

Although no figures can be found, it would seem safe to assume

The Chinese 9 mm Type 59 pistol, a Chinese copy of the Soviet PM.

that the numbers of PM pistols in use around the world exceeds the totals of any other model. They are sound, unremarkable pistols, but they meet to perfection the three main Soviet requirements for a service weapon. They are designed for mass production, they are extremely robust, and they will seemingly be around for ever.

SMITH & WESSON 645

Nation of origin: USA
Ammunition: .45 ACP
Operation: short recoil
Weight: empty, 1.063 kg
Length: 219 mm
Length of barrel: 127 mm
Magazine capacity: 8 rounds
Muzzle velocity: approx. 255 m/s

As will be repeated in the following entry, the name Smith &
Wesson is synonymous with revolvers, but they have also produced
automatic pistols. The first mass-produced Smith & Wesson
automatics were small and unremarkable 'pocket pistols' produced during the 1920s; they made little impact on the market. During the 1950s Smith & Wesson made another attempt to produce
automatics and introduced a series of pistols (the Model 39) based on the use of the 9 mm Parabellum cartridge. These pistols were
good, sound designs with little of note technically, other than that
they attempted to introduce the 9 mm Parabellum round into the
American market.

It was to prove an uphill struggle. The .45 ACP cartridge had
for long been established as the preferred round for all military

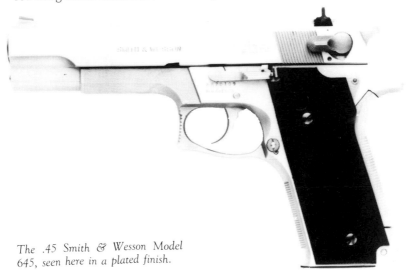

*The .45 Smith & Wesson Model
645, seen here in a plated finish.*

and heavy police work in the United States ever since the Colt M1911 and M1911A1 automatics became the standard American service pistol just before the First World War. Since then, the Colt M1911 pistols had become a virtual legend, to the point where replacing them usually meant rebuilding worn-out examples. The Americans came to be .45 and M1911-minded to such a degree that any mention of a replacement design was met with almost violent reaction. Thus the big American pistol manufacturers grew complacent, while their designs were gradually being overtaken by technical innovations introduced elsewhere. Although Colt and Smith & Wesson did not immediately appreciate it, matters got to the point where even their new models were becoming outdated. Thus when Smith & Wesson produced their Model 39 in 1954, it was technically very little advanced compared with the M1911; even the locking mechanism used a derivative short recoil design.

The 9 mm Smith & Wesson Model 639.

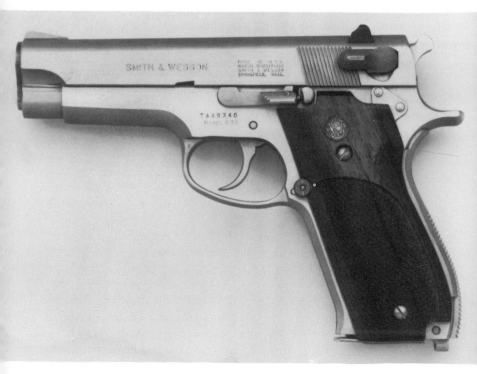

The 9 mm Smith & Wesson Model 459 with its distinctive rear-sight 'ears'; this model was the one initially entered by Smith & Wesson for the US Army's XM9 selection contest.

The fact that it fired a 9 mm Parabellum cartridge did little to improve its sales prospects. A few batches were sold to some American police forces, but the most important sales sere to US Navy Sea Air Land Teams (the SEALS) who purchased Model 39s fitted with silencers. Since the intended targets were supposed to be 'enemy' watch-dogs, these pistols are known colloquially as 'Hush Puppies'. The Model 39 was replaced in production during 1970 by the Model 59, which was little more than the Model 39 revised to accommodate 15 rounds in place of the eight rounds of the earlier model.

Smith & Wesson's advocacy of the 9 mm Parabellum cartridge did have some success, in that it brought home to the American military authorities the fact that there was a viable alternative to the venerable .45 cartridge. The US Air Force ordered Smith & Wesson automatics in some numbers and this drew the 9 mm calibre to the attention of the US Army planners – their counterparts in Europe were already well aware of the ascendancy of the 9 mm Parabellum round. In time, this led to the issuing of the XM9

pistol specification (mentioned in more detail in the entry on the
Beretta Model 92 F). Smith & Wesson decided to enter the XM9
contest and developed a version of the Model 59 known as the
Model 459. There were several slight variations on the theme of
the Model 459, but they all had one thing in common - they were
eliminated from the initial XM9 contest for one reason or another.
Not to be outdone, Smith & Wesson came up with the Model
459M, supposedly with all the shortcomings of the earlier model
put right - or so they thought, for their entry was no more successful during the second run of the XM9 contest than it had been
in the first.

It was all a bit much for Smith & Wesson, who promptly started
making various legal moves and threatening dire consequences if
the contract award to Beretta was not rescinded. They were not
successful, despite considerable string-pulling in the Senate and
Congress and, although it means jumping the sequence somewhat,
the end result was that the honoured house of Smith & Wesson
was taken over by a British financial coup. (At the time of writing
there was still an outside chance that there would be another M9
pistol 'shoot off', even though Beretta are already producing their
Model 92F.)

The XM9 contest was not a complete fiasco for Smith & Wesson,
for from the Model 459M came the Model 659 which was ordered
by various security agencies. (The '6' in the designation denotes
that the pistol is constructed using stainless steel, a material that
is becoming increasingly popular in pistol manufacturing circles.)
However, the Model 659 was deemed to be rather bulky to meet
a potential requirement by US Air Force. The result was the Model
469, which is a smaller version of the Model 459 used for the XM9
programme. This model continues to use the 9 mm Parabellum
cartridge and has a light alloy frame coupled with a steel slide. One
unusual feature is that the double-action has no spur, full reliance
being placed upon the double-action trigger mechanism.

In another attempt to recoup something from the XM9 contest,
Smith & Wesson decided to virtually throw in the towel by producing a .45 ACP version of the Model 659, thereby turning the
wheel full circle. The result is the Model 645 which is now in production.

It is easy for the armchair pundit to make comments without
responsibility, but in many ways the very emergence of the Model
645 marks the current ascendancy of the European pistol design

bureaux. There is little present in the Model 645 that would be unfamiliar to the producers of the old Colt Model 1911. The overall appearance of the weapon is very similar to the Colt veteran and many of the technical aspects, such as the various safeties, are essentially similar, although an automatic safety has been introduced to prevent firing unless the trigger is definitely pulled. There are none of the super-safeties of the European pistols, and the breech locking system is virtually identical to that of many earlier models.

The ammunition is also a return to old values. Designed from the outset to fire a bullet that would stop a running man at close ranges, the powerful .45 ACP cartridge has also proved to be too much of a good thing. The .45 ACP cartridge produces a fearsome report on firing, and the resultant recoil forces are such that only pistols as hefty as the M1911 or Model 645 can fire it with safety. The result is a pistol that terrifies raw recruits and requires careful and prolonged training to use efficiently. Experienced pistol enthusiasts may delight in firing heavy calibre pistols, but the average combat user is rarely a pistol enthusiast.

The Model 645 does possess some modern touches. The trigger guard has the reversed arc over its forward portion to accommodate the double-handed firing grip, while the safety catch is ambidextrous. One small and thoughtful feature is the bevelling around the magazine slot that assists in guiding a loaded box magazine into the butt. Another nice touch is the numbering along the magazine to denote the number of rounds remaining. There is also a Model 745 which is a 'super-finished' pistol, intended only for the upper echelons of the pistol enthusiast market.

SMITH & WESSON MODEL 29

Nation of origin: USA
Ammunition: .44 Magnum
Weight: empty with 165 mm barrel, 1.332 kg
Length: with 165 mm barrel, 302 mm
Length of barrel: 101, 165 or 212 mm
Cylinder capacity: 6 rounds
Muzzle velocity: approx. 440 m/s

The name Smith & Wesson is synonymous with revolvers. Although Colt produced the first sucessful examples, Smith & Wesson gradually became the market leaders in the United States, and for revolvers that meant the rest of the world as well. Over the decades, the list of numbers and models produced has grown to an enormous total. Even today, the list of models on offer is so extensive that only the most specialized requirement will not be met by at least one model currently in the catalogue.

The number of revolvers on offer from Smith & Wesson covers calibres from the small to the most powerful cartridges commercially available. The list of intended purposes ranges from target pistols to undisguised man-stoppers. Nearly all revolvers from the Smith & Wesson stable use the same basic construction. They have a steel frame, inside which rotates a cylinder holding the rounds to be fired. For loading and

The .44 Magnum Smith & Wesson Model 29, one of the most powerful handguns available.

A close rival to the Smith & Wesson Model 29 is the Ruger Redhawk, a revolver available in a number of Magnum calibres and with a number of possible barrel lengths.

unloading, the cylinder swings out to the left under the control of a release catch, also on the left of the frame. Trigger mechanisms may be single action (now rarely used outside target pistols) or double action, the latter being by far the most common. Actions may have exposed or completely shrouded hammers. Barrel lengths vary enormously from the diminutive to the lengthy, and the number of types of grip vary from the custom-made to those that seem to have been stuck on as an after-thought.

One thing these revolvers nearly all have in common is that they are rarely used for military purposes. The main output of Smith & Wesson, apart from sales to the public at large, goes to police and security forces. Into this bracket fall the main military users, namely military police and other military security and guard organizations. The reasons for these continuing sales to the police when the military are now automatic pistol orientated require a little examination.

Taking the military police as an example, some form of weapon has to be provided during the course of many military policing duties. Most of the time it is inappropriate or difficult to carry a weapon as bulky or obvious as a rifle, but a pistol carried in a belt holster is an innocuous way of being armed effectively enough to meet most eventualities. Most military policemen will thankfully acknowledge that there are few occasions for them to actually draw their pistols in anger. They will then go on to say that when they do need to use their pistols, they need to use them quickly. Revolvers can be carried in holsters for extended periods in a perfectly safe state, yet can be ready to fire as soon as they are drawn and as soon as the trigger is pressed. Only the latest

Revolvers such as the .44 Magnum Ruger Super Redhawk are rarely encountered in use as military weapons and are really meant for the sporting shooter.

automatic pistol designs can claim to meet such a specification.

When they are not required, revolvers need, and usually get, few attentions other than routine cleaning. They are inherently strong and can withstand the hard and constant knocks that seem to come with prolonged security duties and, once loaded, are ready for immediate duty at any time.

One aspect of the modern combat pistol where the revolver scores over the automatic is in the use of Magnum ammunition. The Magnum cartridge grew out of the American predeliction for hand-loading ever more powerful cartridges to fire from ever more powerful hand guns. This requirement for powerful cartridges was met commercially by the introduction of the .357, .41 and .44 Magnum cartridges. All three are so powerful that for most intents and purposes, only revolvers can have the inherent strength in their frames to handle the stresses produced on firing - the firer has to handle the recoil forces himself. Coverage has been given elsewhere to the problems such powerful rounds can introduce to military users, but the Magnums have attractions for specialized police units. There are already enough indications from the media and entertainments industry to demonstrate that there is a strata of society that is so violent that only the most drastic methods of stopping their unlawful actions will suffice. This has given rise to the 'Dirty Harry' syndrome in some American police circles, and they have demanded weapons to match their determination to stop the actions of even the most determined wrongdoer.

The result has been one of the most powerful handguns currently available commercially. This is the Smith & Wesson Model 29 firing the .44 Magnum cartridge, *the* Dirty Harry gun. Anyone hit with the projectile from such a weapon will definitely take no further interest in subsequent proceedings, for the striking power of a blunt-nosed bullet from a .44 Magnum cartridge is enough to lift a grown man off his feet and move him several feet, even at ranges of 25 metres or more.

The very sight of a Model 29 is impressive. It is a large and handsome revolver with a sizeable frame. The cylinder holds six rounds and the user has the choice of using single or double trigger action. Various forms of sight can be used; some target-shooting enthusiasts use optical sights and some extremists even use a telescopic sight and Model 29 combination for big game hunting. Three barrel lengths are available to suit customer requirements. The longer barrels provide the better accuracy at long ranges, which can be well over 50 metres in the hands of a skilled user.

And that is the rub; only the most experienced and well-trained user can get the best out of a weapon such as the Model 29. Even before firing, it is a massive handful. On firing, the Model 29 produces a recoil that will throw the firer's arm over his head unless he is in exactly the correct firing pose (head down, knees bent, arms extended, etc.) and uses the two-handed grip. There is also the problem of carrying such a large pistol about the person. That may be regarded as a minor problem, for many users of weapons such as the Model 29 will be happy for all to know that such a weapon is being carried. The very sight of a Model 29 is enough to make any potential felon think twice!

RUGER P-85

Nation of origin: USA
Ammunition: 9 x 19 mm
Operation: short recoil
Weight: loaded, 1.08 kg
Length: 199 mm
Length of barrel: 114.3 mm
Magazine capacity: 15 rounds
Muzzle velocity: approx. 350 m/s

Without a doubt, the most important single event to have taken place on the combat pistol scene over the last few decades has been the US Army's M9 pistol selection contest. One of the less expected aspects of the contest programme was that although the US Army issued some very demanding specifications for the competition, all the entrants were either already-existing designs, or modifications of existing designs produced to meet the specifications. No completely original design was involved.

However, one had been expected, even though it did not materialize until well after the Beretta 92F had been announced as the successful M9 candidate. The expected entry duly emerged as the Ruger P-85. Its late arrival on the American pistol scene was unfortunate, for the P-85 looks like being a weapon to put American pistol design back on an even par with the European manufacturers. If the P-85 had taken part in the M9 contest, the eventual outcome might have been different.

Sturm, Ruger and Company of Southport, Connecticut, entered the small arms market during 1949, and although their first products were small-calibre sporting automatics, they really made their name with a series of revolvers. They overcame the existing market domination of Colt and Smith & Wesson by going back to revolver design fundamentals and virtually redesigning the revolver from scratch. By using modern materials such as high grade stainless steel (the use of which has become a virtual Ruger trademark), producing revised frames to enable even the most powerful Magnum cartridges to be fired, and by introducing foolproof safety devices, Ruger revolvers soon became market leaders. Both single- and double-action revolvers have been produced (including a best-selling direct copy of the old single action Colt 'Peacemaker', chambered for the .22 long rifle cartridge) culminating in the 'Redhawk' series of revolvers produced to fire the Magnum rounds ~ the .44 Magnum Redhawk and Super Redhawk rival the Smith & Wesson Model 29 as being the most powerful handguns available.

When news began to leak out that Ruger were to produce a sevice automatic, its arrival was awaited eagerly by many. It duly appeared in early 1987 under the name of Ruger P-85, and soon demonstrated that it was well worth the wait. In short, the P-85 embodies most of the features that have become commonplace in designs produced outside the United States, and adds a few innovations of its own, not the least important of which is a relatively low purchase price compared to many other contemporary pistols.

Ruger have publicly denied that the P-85 was designed with the M9 specification in mind, but almost every aspect of the P-85 meets the M9 specification with an exactitude that cannot be coincidental, right down to the provision of a lanyard loop on the butt. It is a good-looking weapon, with the frame using a precision investment casting in lightweight aluminium alloy which has been hardened for toughness. The slide is made using high-grade heat-treated chrome-molybdenum steel. Slide and frame are both finished in matt black. The butt grip panels use a hard nylon-based material known as 'Xenoy' that provides a

The clean modern lines of the 9 mm Ruger P-85.

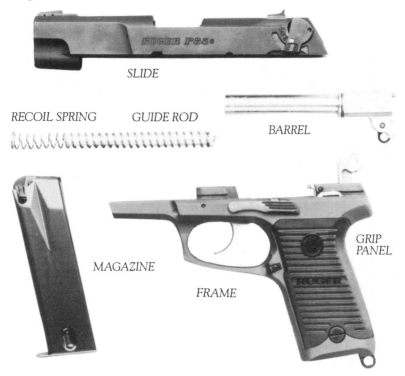

SLIDE

RECOIL SPRING   GUIDE ROD

BARREL

MAGAZINE

FRAME

GRIP
PANEL

Left *9 mm Ruger P-85 in its lockable carrying case.*

Above *The main components of the 9 mm Ruger P-85.*

comfortable non-slip hold.

When considering the detail of the P-85, there is much to examine. Starting with the trigger mechanism, a double-action system is used, but allied to a trigger with a more than usually pronounced curve to aid the pull when a full cocking and firing action is required. The trigger guard is larger than normal, to enable firing operations with gloved hands to be accomplished with ease - many contemporary pistol designs overlook this simple requirement. The trigger guard also has the now commonplace reversed arc for the double-grip firing grip.

The safety catch is ambidextrous to enable both right- and left-handed users to handle the pistol without difficulty. When the safety catch (located at the end of the slide) is in the 'safe' position, the firing pin is blocked from moving forward, the hammer is blocked from contacting the firing pin and in addition the entire firing mechanism is disconnected from the trigger. As with so many other designs, the P-85 employs the short recoil locking system, but in place of the usual barrel lug that rests in a lug on the slide, the chamber end of the barrel has a square section. This squared-off section locks into the ejection opening of the slide but otherwise the locking mechanism acts in the manner of the Colt-Browning tilting barrel.

The magazine release catch can be operated from either side of the pistol, and the pistol can be loaded with the safety catch on 'safe'. Ruger have claimed that the slide and barrel design has been optimized to prevent jamming. If a malfunction should occur it can be cleared readily without difficulty and such is the design detail present on the P-85 that individual rounds can be easily chambered by hand. This latter operation is theoretically possible on many other pistols, but in practice is far from simple to accomplish.

The sights are provided with white dot inserts to enable aiming to be as quick and easy as possible, even in poor lighting conditions; the rear sight is adjustable for windage. Field stripping can be carried out without tools, and all parts, even the smallest, are robust to withstand the sort of damage that can be inflicted unwittingly on such components when removed from their intended locations. The overall strength of the P-85 has been demonstrated by a series of proof-testings during which a P-85 fired 10,000 rounds without any breakages and without any appreciable signs of wear.

If the Ruger P-85 has one fault that has been demonstrated to date, it is that few have yet to be seen in the hands of purchasers. Even allowing for the fact that to set up any sort of production line takes time, the slow appearance of production P-85s is worthy of remark. Ruger had plans to mass produce P-85s in an entirely new plant that would operate almost entirely under computer control. The most likely reason for the delay appears to be that some minor technical hitch has become apparent, and Ruger are using their considerable expertise to ensure that any such hitch is eliminated entirely before commencing production.

ASP

Nation of origin: USA
Ammunition: 9 x 19 mm
Operation: short recoil
Weight: loaded, 0.652 kg
Length: 188 mm
Length of barrel: 57 mm
Magazine capacity: 7 rounds
Muzzle velocity: approx. 340 m/s

One aspect of the American pistol scene is the vast number of 'custom built' pistols that can be found on the open market. These custom-builds vary from the slight alterations introduced for or by the pistol buff, to extensive re-makes of commercial models that have been carried out either to suit a user philosophy or in attempts to 'gild the lily' to some degree or other. The pistol that has been the main subject of the custom builders' attention has for long been the venerable Colt 0.45 M1911 and M1911A1. The conversions and modifications relating to this pistol have been legion, and every year some new

The 9 mm Smith & Wesson Model 39, the starting point for the ASP conversion.

form of alteration or accessory is offered.

An examination of these various embellishments to existing designs would fill this book many times over; the reader is recommended to peruse the small ad section of pistol enthusiast magazines to gain an idea of the selection of goods on offer. Some of the modifications or accessories are, to use the vernacular, strictly for the birds, and one can only wonder at the optimism that led to their being placed on the market. Others are more important, for they can alter the very role that a particular pistol design has to play. To provide an example of this, one can go back to the Second World War when Colt Woodsman .22 sporting pistols were converted to undercover resistance weapons by the addition of silencers.

That example entailed but a simple modification. Many of the custom-builds produced over the years have been what can only be described at complete rebuilds of weapons. Such an example can be seen in the conversion of a Smith & Wesson 9 mm Model 39 pistol into the ASP. The original Model 39 is a service pistol, pure and simple. The ASP cannot be described as anything other than a concealed weapon designed for close combat.

The philosophy that produced the ASP is worth investigation. Many police and other security agencies use undercover or plain clothes agents, who often have to operate under conditions that involve considerable personal risk. Such conditions often mean that some form of easily-concealed weapon has to be carried, and when that weapon is drawn is has to be used rapidly to produce as many shots on target as possible. This specification entails rather more than just small dimensions. It requires that no part of the pistol will snag on clothing as it is drawn (something all too prone to happen using conventional pistols), that the weapon fits easily into the hand and that when the pistol is fired the operation is smooth and rapid. All these specifications are met by the ASP.

The ASP conversion is carried out by Armaments Systems and Procedures Incorporated (hence ASP) of Appleton, Wisconsin. They produce what is virtually a new weapon from a Smith & Wesson Model 39. The original pistol is taken down to its constituent parts and rebuilt. All the exterior parts are ground down to provide a really smooth outline, and are then coated with Teflon to make the outline smoother still. Even the grips, of which more later, are smooth. The idea is that even if the user is

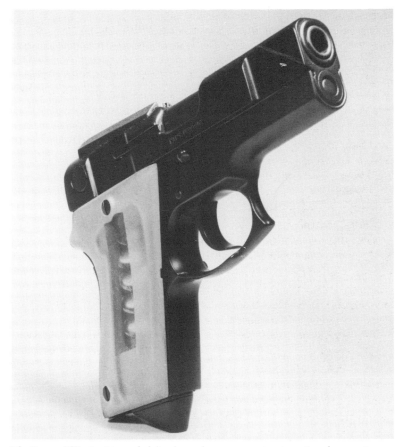

The 9 mm ASP pistol intended for the undercover security operative; the transparent butt grips are readily apparent, but less obvious is the Guttersnipe sighting system over the receiver.

in a near-panic state, the usual pistol grip will enable the pistol to assume its natural position in the hand to assist in accurate aiming of the all-important first shot.

The rest of the pistol assembly involves hand fitting of virtually every part. A new recoil spring is fitted and every part is reground and rebushed. Particular attention is given to assembling the trigger mechanism, which results in its being capable of very rapid rates of fire. The rapid fire mode is a particular feature of the ASP, and the makers claim that cyclic rates of up to 300 rounds a minute are possible. Note that this is not automatic fire, but deliberate individual movements of the trigger. This involves the use of a two-handed grip with firing stability provided by the addition of a magazine extension that accommodates a little finger to provide extra grip under the butt. To speed up magazine changing in combat situations, the Model 39 magazine safety that usually prevents firing with the box magazine extracted has been removed. This enables a round to be left in the chamber ready to fire as the magazine is removed and replaced.

The ASP does not use conventional sights. Instead it has a typical product from the American pistol accessory market in the form of the Guttersnipe sight. The Guttersnipe is one of those simple ideas that are far from simple to produce in usable form, but which are soon grasped once seen and utilized. There is only one part to the sight, which has a long slot cut into a single piece of metal. As the user looks along the slot the three sides (the two sides and bottom) form a symmetrical pattern when the pistol is aimed. Any imbalance of any particular side (or sides) will indicate an incorrect aim. The main attributes of the Guttersnipe are that it is extremely easy and quick to use, and provides more than adequate accuracy at combat ranges. There are none of the usual difficulties involved in lining up a target, fore sight and rear sight. To add to its advantages, the outline of the Guttersnipe is smooth and low. It should be emphasized that the Guttersnipe is a combat sight for use at close ranges. It is not a target-shooting sight.

The Guttersnipe is not the only novelty featured on the ASP. Again the innovation is simple but invaluable in a combat situation, for one of the butt grips has a transparent slot along its entire length to allow the user to see exactly how many rounds are left to fire at any time. The ASP is supplied with three magazines and it is recommended that half-empty magazines are replaced whenever an opportunity arises during a combat situation. The two spare magazines can be carried in a special double magazine holder located on a belt or somewhere about the person.

The makers of ASP lay considerable emphasis on the selection of the 9 x 19 mm Parabellum ammunition used with the weapon. Since the ASP is meant to be used in situations that can only be described as desperate, any misfires caused by faulty or poor quality ammunition could be potentially fatal. The makers specify that surplus military ammunition should not be used, and state that full jacketed ammunition, such as that produced for some sub-machine guns, performs best, even if soft pointed lead bullets are usually deemed better for anti-personnel use at short ranges.

The ASP is a highly specialized form of combat pistol, but it does provide an excellent example of how existing designs can be modified to suit particular requirements. Any would-be owner of an ASP should, however, be warned that they are extremely unlikely to own one. Quite apart from the high cost involved (the initial Model 39 has to be paid for before all the conversion work is even considered, and it will be appreciated that the work is time-consuming and involved), ASPs are produced to cater for a particular need in a precisely-defined market. Sales to prospective purchasers outside that bracket will not normally be considered.

The ASP is not a pistol that is likely to be commonly encountered, but it is a very interesting approach to a particular aspect of modern combat pistol design.

INDEX